# BECOMING ONE

By

Femi Alaran

Published by Femi Alaran
British Library Cataloguing Data
A catalogue record of this book is available from the British Library

To obtain further copies or contact author:
Website: **www.LITWIC.org** E mail: **contactus@litwic.org**
Printed in England

# Dedication

*I dedicate this book to my wife,*
*the flesh of my flesh and*
*the bone of my bone.*

*Thank you for*
*always being there for me*

# Acknowledgement

The success of any project depends mostly on the encouragement and effort of many others. I take this opportunity to express my gratitude to the people who have been instrumental in the successful completion of this book. I want to show my highest appreciation to the Almighty God for the grace and help in the conclusion of this work.

My special thanks go to my wife, who has been a pillar of support throughout the completion of this manuscript. I want to express my gratitude to all members of my family for their understanding and help in completing this work.

My thanks go to countless men and women of God, who I benefited from their ministries and words of Wisdom. I am particularly grateful to our pre-marital counsellors, Pastor O. J. Kuye, and Pastor Anthony Ashaye. My gratitude to the people who have counselled me on the institution of marriage, and the lessons they've learnt in their marriages.

I would like to appreciate every author whose work I have cited in this book, countless men and women of God across the globe, who I have been a beneficiary of their ministry and gifts.

My thanks go to my proof-reader who edited the manuscript in a professional and timely manner. My Special thanks to the cover designer for excellent Graphic work.

I am very grateful to all.

Thank you

Femi Alaran

# Acknowledgements

# Contents

# Introduction

"Eeny, meeny, miny, moe," choosing a mate is supposed to be easy. Our Education System prepares us for an excellent work-life but fails to teach us any principles about love. Many people have gone on to have very successful careers professionally but have failed in their marriages. A man once exclaimed, "I am not doing that again," after his fourth marriage ended in a divorce. You would have thought he'd have learnt his lesson after the first marriage. The current statistics show 50 percent of first-time marriages will end in divorce; most people think their marriage will be the exception to the current trend. The wedding day is often spectacular if only the happily after was the same.

Great marriages are built on excellent marital education. It isn't easy to pass an exam if you haven't prepared for it. We all have a different school of thought when it comes to love; you might hear different one-liners like, "All you need is love," "Good communication is key to success in marriage," "A family that prays together stays together," "Don't buy it till you try it," etc. These myths and unrealistic expectations about marriage have enabled so many young adults to walk to the altar with both eyes shut. In some cases, it has left many young attractive men and women single for a very long time because they are waiting for that perfect person. Some people are their own worst enemy when it comes to getting married; they put themselves under undue pressure. The anxiety they create for themselves clouds their judgment; their source of information is soap operas, wedding magazines, movies, girls talk, boys talk, relatives, parents, pastors, etc.

Falling in love is easy, but staying in love is a different thing entirely. You need to carefully evaluate your similarities, differences, values, goals, and aspirations with your partner. A relationship based on hormones and feelings is dangerous and often leaves one party short-changed. The decision to marry is based on both emotion and objective; in other words, your head and heart. If the scales are tilted too far to one side, it causes challenges. The ability to have a healthy, loving relationship requires paying attention to details. Failed relationships happen for many reasons and a source of great pain and sorrow to the parties involved.

This book is about preparing you for marriage, but it is very different from your typical self-help books. First, I aim to identify what premarital factors can predict the success of a marriage. If you are in a serious relationship, you need to answer the question of whether or not you should pursue marriage with your partner. We begin our journey in this book by evaluating our person, assets, and liabilities. It is easy to blame everyone for your love challenges, from your parents to your exes but not yourself. Secondly, how ready are you to get married? Often couples ignore key topics until it is too late, like money, relationship cycle, underlying health issues, education status, etc. Thirdly, we look at your conflict management skills. If your parent's marriage is your role model, then most likely, their conflict management style has been transferred to you.

In some cases, your parent marital dissatisfaction has affected you emotionally on how to resolve conflict without resulting to underhand tactics. You have to understand that maturity is not to be postponed until you are in a relationship. If you go into a relationship and you haven't worked on you, what you will do is begin to try to work on the other person (see Luke 6:4. If we haven't dealt adequately with our issues when we are single, we will carry our challenges into our relationship. We will also refocus our attention on the other person's problems; this is the cause of many conflicts in a relationship.

A relationship brings together two different mindsets and moulds them into one. The process of getting to know your partner takes many years of incremental steps. It's essential to know and understand; it is a process, and processes take time. There must be a willingness from both parties to acknowledge mistakes and weaknesses; this will help considerably to manage the ups and downs that come with a relationship. Most couples go into a relationship with unrealistic expectations engulfed in emotional attraction. It's wise to get to know the other person before making a commitment that's painful and difficult to undo. Dating without a purpose is like going to the market to test drive a car without the intention of buying it. You have wasted your time and that of the car dealer. There is a cost associated with dating. If there is no real purpose to your dating, it will be a waste of your resources and time. A date should be an opportunity for you to assess the suitability of the other person for marriage. You should date with the expectation of getting to know who God has created this person to be, before you dream of the next ten years with the person. Bear in mind that the other person is free to walk away whether he or she is a Christian or not. Likewise, if you're not interested in pursuing the relationship, be honest and let the other person know sooner rather than later. It may hurt either way, but it will hurt a lot less early than it will later.

I pray that you discover God's truth about relationships through the pages of this book.

# CHAPTER 1

## *Who are you?*

This simple question has enormous implications; a vast majority of young adults will not be able to articulate who they are in few sentences. The first step toward marital success is to define who you are clearly. It will save you time, resources, energy, and heartbreaks from kissing a lot of frogs in the process of trying to find a suitable mate. Marriage is for two mature individuals who are ready for a lifelong commitment to one another. It's not for Babies known for crying and screaming at the top of their voices to get attention, but unable to articulate their desires when they get the attention they seek. You have to know yourself well enough to be able to express your desired needs in a relationship.

If I was to ask you, "Who are you?" The most common response I would get is "My name is John Doe," "I am a Christian," or "I am the bank manager," assuming I met you at your place of work. Our identity goes beyond being able to recite our names in a moments' notice, or description of our occupation, or religious affiliation. We often fall into the trap of using our name or job description to define ourselves. Your identity gives you a sense of wholeness. If you define yourself by your career, and you lose your job at some point in your life, you might lose your identity with it. You can introduce yourself by your name or occupation, but you cannot define yourself by it. Your identity is a combination of various factors in your life - your name, gender, ethnic, race, experiences, education, occupation, belief, values, likes, dislikes, strengths, weaknesses, vision, goals, life aspirations, etc. Until you can clearly define who you are, it is unfair and unrealistic to expect your future partner to meet your needs in the relationship. Each of these factors provides us with the source of our identity. Once we understand who we are, we can avoid many of the pitfalls in life.

Identity crisis is a significant topic within the body of Christ. The first temptation of Jesus was about his identity (see Matthew 4:1-3). Knowing how unique you are, helps greatly in your self-esteem; meaning you are not willing to sell yourself cheaply. Do you know that you were born a winner out of potentially millions of candidates vying for one egg? How is it that you got to the egg, and the others did not? You are a miracle, and you must celebrate that. God saw tremendous potential in each of us before any of us could tell the difference between our left and right hand. We came into this world with a plan and a purpose (see Jeremiah 29:11), but God has given us the option of whether or not we would fulfill that plan. The choices we make today makes all the differences in what life is going to be like tomorrow (see Deuteronomy 30:19). One of the most common reasons we choose the wrong partner is that we do not know who we are and what we want. It is hard to choose someone who is capable of meeting your needs and shares the same values as you when you have not developed the skills or confidence to voice out your needs and boundaries. I recommend that you take a personality test to identify what are your strengths and weaknesses. What you would bring to the table in a relationship, and then, quite possibly, you can transform your weaknesses to strength. It is advisable not to pretend to be something or someone you are not. So many people have become actors and actresses in the movie called life. Some people have gone as far as wearing a mask and costume to portray a character, but for how long would you keep up appearances. However, being an actor or actress is not necessarily a bad thing. Daily we all play a role. For example, we all have to act professionally at work - imagine you work in a department store, you are expected to smile at your customer when they walk in and be polite even if you feel provoked by them. The challenge is, people become a character, after playing the role for so long; we cannot separate reality from fiction. In essence, we are hiding behind a mask, pretending to be someone we are not. Trouble begins when we perpetuate a role until we perceive it as truth and deceive even ourselves. So, I ask again, who are you?

## WHY DO YOU WANT TO GET MARRIED?

The most straightforward answer is love. Falling in love is one thing, but staying in love is another. There is a significant number of young adults who are battling with loneliness in our fast-paced society. Being married is part of our culture; the stigma of being single might raise concerns from friends and family who expected you to be married at a certain age. Their expectations generate unwanted questions, though they mean well, and it creates pressure and sometimes makes us feel inadequate. Some Christians believe all of their problems stem from being single because they define their self-worth by their marital status. They make statements like, "I can't make any permanent plans until I get married." A single man or woman has the opportunity to develop a well-balanced life that can be a support system for years to come. Being single is a gift that can shape us into the person God wants us to be (see 1 Corinthians 7:33-35). It is not a curse or punishment to be single, nor is it a trial to be endured. Being single creates the right set of circumstances to grow in other relationships we have in our lives, especially with our Saviour, Jesus. When a person focuses their attention on getting to know the Lord more intimately, they will not struggle with rejection, low self-esteem, anxiety, or bitterness. One of the reasons God instituted marriage was to show humans the kind of relationship He wants to have with every person on the earth. In the New Testament, the analogy is Christ as the Bridegroom, and the Church is His Bride. Marriage is about being able to live in harmony, commonality, and agreement, which is impossible when you don't know who you are. Are you indeed a Christian or merely playing church?

If you are yet to discover who you are, it will not be easy to make a success of your romantic relationship. You might have convinced yourself of different reasons why you need to be married, and some of these reasons might be genuine. For example, a lady might want to marry because of her age as she approaches the end of her fertility cycle. However, other reasons are questionable, such as trying to get even with an ex-partner, or you want to put on a wedding dress. Your identity is important; being able to define who you are and who you are not, is crucial to the success of the relationship. God emphasizes individuality, the first thing He gave to Man, is His image and likeness (see Genesis 1:26). Without a true definition of your identity, you are easily swayed by the opinion of others about you, your self-worth or your value fluctuates with the view of others. Marriage is a commitment to each other despite knowing each other's faults and failings; it should not change according to the weather or the environment.

## PERSONALITY TEST – THE FRUIT OF THE SPIRIT

*"But the fruit of the Spirit is love, joy, peace, forbearance, kindness, goodness, faithfulness, gentleness, and self-control. Against such things, there is no law."* (Galatians 5:22-23)

One of the reasons often cited for marital break down is irreconcilable differences due to different personality traits. Some people are talkers, while others are more reserved. Some people are very organized, while others are less concerned about things around them. It can be frustrating at times when people with different personality traits get together. Their disagreements often stem from having opposite points of view and not because one person is right, and the other person is wrong. Different personalities add spice to life and provide us with different perspectives and ideas as we live together. For example, a big dreamer needs someone who is detailed oriented. God has made humans inter-dependant, and this is one of the beauties of humanity.

Let me share a story with you; James was stunned to find himself in the middle of a divorce just two years after his fairy-tale wedding to Jane. No one could have predicted the events; the soon to be ex-couple were a match made in heaven while the marriage lasted, Jane and James were in love with each other. Jane would often brag to her friends about how incredible James was. He frequently bought her roses, opened doors, and helped with the chores around the house. He was perfect, so what went wrong?

Jane is a lawyer who excelled in her profession, and James is a handsome chef with excellent culinary skills. She earns more money than her husband as a corporate lawyer. The couple met while Jane was out celebrating with her colleagues after closing a big deal with a major client in a restaurant where James worked as the head chef. He was charming to Jane throughout the evening. James went the extra mile throughout the evening, and they both felt some chemistry between them. By the end of the evening, they had exchanged numbers, and within a few months of dating, they were walking down the church aisle to say, "I do."

Over time their differences started to spring to light. The initial chemistry seemed to have faded. James wasn't interested in a long logical argument. He often felt overwhelmed and lost in the process. Jane, on the other hand, enjoyed a dialogue backed with solid reasoning. James felt threatened by Jane, continually trying to prove a point and always wanting to win an argument. To top it off, Jane felt the need to correct his choice of words and grammar. He felt belittled, being the rightful head of the home. The couple began to drift apart, and resentment grew between them. They were now seeking separation from each other.

Humans are not magnets; opposites don't attract. The ability to have a healthy, loving relationship requires paying attention to details. We are often under the impression that falling in love will automatically build a great relationship that will lead to a good marriage. Falling in love is the result of two people connecting on an emotional level. This type of emotional chemistry allows the love birds involved, to spend hours on the phone without saying anything meaningful. Their heart almost skips a beat when the other person walks into the room. Their mind is always, all day long, thinking about the other person, and they can't wait to receive a phone call or text message from them. It creates some pressure for physical intimacy before they even know each other well enough. The truth is most people don't know themselves well enough to articulate their needs or wants in a relationship.

Psychologists have identified four main personality traits, which are Sanguine, Choleric, Melancholic, and Phlegmatic. Our personality traits reflect characteristic patterns of thoughts, feelings, and behaviours. As Christians, our personality should be grounded in the Holy Spirit. The standard by which we measure our maturity is the fruit of the Spirit. How ripe is the fruit of the Spirit in your life? Note; it is fruit and not fruits, indicating singular. Your development of one aspect of the fruit does not excuse or negate lack of growth in another, and kindness does not trump self-control. When you look closely at the fruit of the Spirit, you notice they are relational. It reveals our relationships with other people. Ask married couples; they're forced every day to put the fruit of the Spirit into practice. You can't hide in a marriage, the authentic you will come out. Marriage is relationships where partners see the best and worst in each other. Many of us would like to have somebody willing to be patient with us, even with our flaws and quirks. Patience means that they will not put you under pressure to make a decision or to do something you feel uncomfortable doing. They will give you as much time as you need to decide without trying to rush you into something in an attempt to make you feel guilty, especially when it comes to intimacy.

In some relationships, couples blame each other for their shortcomings but fail to recognise that the fault lies with them. All relationships require work; by developing the fruit of the Spirit in your life, you're getting a head start. If you still find yourself easily angered or keeping malice, it shows that there is an aspect to the fruit you have yet to develop. Love is not easily angered; you can't claim to be in love and have a record of wrongdoings. The sooner you recognise these tendencies, the better it is, and the more fruitful your future relationship can be. Remember that the smallest decisions today can become a life-changing event. We must strive individually to develop ourselves to be the best we can be. I would recommend that every person should take a test of the fruit of the Spirit to see how we measure against each aspect of the fruit. Relationships require a willingness to be changed by the spirit of God. God will keep the chemistry alive in any relationship, so long as we open our hearts to loving each other in the way He determined it.

## WHAT LOVE LANGUAGE DO YOU SPEAK?

I read a book by Gary Chapman, titled "The Five Love Languages." I will recommend this book to all couples. In this book, the author explained how to discover our love languages and how to use it to connect with our partner; this helps us to find out who we are, what you bring to the table, and how we express and receive love. With this insight, we are equipped to communicate love to others effectively. He categorised the Love Languages under five headings:

**Physical Touch:** This is the most direct way to communicate love. It calms and reassures. It could be as simple as holding hands while walking in the park. You're comfortable with public displays of affection, even in front of large groups. Expressions of physical touch don't necessarily lead to intimacy. Partners of people who speak this language must never assume they have permission to touch their significant other at any time or in any place. For this love language to be effective is largely to do with timing.

**Words of Affirmation:** Individuals with this love language need to hear encouraging words of kindness with sincerity in their tone of voice. Words such as, "I love you," "I appreciate you," "Thank you." A pat on the back showing that their effort hasn't gone unnoticed. One of the biggest lies we have been told is "Sticks and stones may break my bones, but words will never hurt me." Words affect us; they put a scar on our soul - some adults still battle with the hurt of the words spoken to them when they were children.

**Gifts:** We all like gifts, but we are affected differently by the gift we receive. The person who loves this language thrives on thoughtfulness. The gift shows that you were thinking about me; actions speak louder than words. "The thing that works best is picking the right gift that shows you understand your partner and the effort you made to express love," says Chapman.

**Quality Time:** This love language is about undivided attention, which means no distraction for TV, Mobile Phone, or the internet. You enjoy spending quality time with your partner. You love the attention you get from your partner. It allows sharing something meaningful, including plans for the future.

**Acts of Service:** Individuals with this love language prefer their partner to be hands-on. To be doing something to ease the burden of responsibility, like vacuuming the floors, asking to do something that relives their pressures, going shopping, or doing the laundry. It doesn't make your partner a slave or your messenger, but it shows that they are thoughtful and willing to go the extra mile for you. Are you this kind of person?

To have your love expectation met in a relationship, you must be able to articulate your love language to your partner. I have witnessed too many couples who expect their partner to be a psychic and know their love language. While some people might be observant, others don't have the skills to deduce their partner's love language. You might have heard the phrase, "Men are from Mars; Women are from Venus." One common mistake is that you might assume your partner likes gifts, and therefore you keep buying them something from the shop. If this is how they express love, that would be great, but if it is not, you might be wasting valuable resources down a black hole that cannot be filled.

# GUIDE YOUR HEART

*"Above all else, guard your heart, for everything you do flows from it."*
(Proverbs 4:23)

Often, we are so fixated on guarding ourselves against physical intimacy in relationships that we neglect the emotional and spiritual components of a relationship, which is equally binding. Emotional intimacy is a beautiful thing in the proper context; you are free to express your thoughts, dreams, and aspirations with the other party without fear or prejudice. But in the wrong context, emotional intimacy can be harmful to our confidence, and self-esteem especially when couples move too fast in a relationship that doesn't translate into anything more than a platonic friendship. It's important that emotional intimacy grows proportionally to the level of commitment from both parties. Falling in love is not worldly; denying your feelings for the opposite sex is not being spiritual. Humans are emotional by nature, but we guard that which has been given to us and "cast our pearls before swine, they would not appreciate it and most likely misuse it." (Matthew 7:6) The challenge most of us have faced in relationships is being able to tell the difference between genuine interest and merely an infatuation. We must be matured enough to say, "I like this person, but I am not moving further until I am sure we are both willing to take the next step." Our emotions should not be run by hope and expectations. Real-life relationships are usually not like what we see in the movies. We must learn to keep our hopes in alignment with reality rather than getting too ahead of ourselves.

Interest occurs when someone is open to the possibility of a relationship with someone they like. Infatuation occurs when someone is obsessed with being with their crush. Interest is a willingness to give a relationship a try if the opportunity presented itself. Infatuation is being fixated on someone when you don't even really know this person that well. Interest is normal.

Margaret Feinberg shared her story on her Blog. She stated an old friend from college popped back into her life. Though he lived on the other side of the country, he started calling three times a week, and sometimes more often. He repeatedly asked to visit, and after putting him off for several months, she finally agreed. The visit went exceptionally well. He met her family, and they had a fabulous time. He continued calling three to four times a week and purchased expensive gifts for holidays. When she planned to run a marathon, he asked if he could fly out to watch and support her. When they went on a long snowshoe adventure, he asked to hold her hand. When she talked about vacation plans, he hinted that he'd like to join her. When they talked about the future, he asked if she'd consider moving to his city. After eight months of this type of behaviour, she finally confessed that she had feelings for him, and he seemed shocked. He just wanted to be friends; she felt naive. Somewhere between the gourmet dinners and flying back and forth across the country, she had interpreted it as something more. His behaviour was tugging on her heartstrings, and because she didn't breach the subject early on, she allowed her emotions to get involved and got hurt.

'Guard your heart' sounds like good advice. But it begs the question, "what am I guarding my heart from? Jesus said, "Do not give dogs what is sacred; do not throw your pearls to pigs. If you do, they may trample them under their feet, and turn and tear you to pieces." (Matthew 7:6) Our emotions sometimes make us act irrationally, often ignoring red flags even when they are staring us in the face. There are no black and white rules when it comes to emotional involvement. It's easier to say "no" to a kiss than to fall in love. Whenever we have something of value, we do all we can to protect it. We might lock it up in a safe or keep it in a safety deposit box at a bank. There is a part of us that God has created that is very valuable, which is our heart. Everything that we do flows out of our hearts, including our salvation (see Romans 10:9 -10).

I learnt the concept of Love Bank from the book by Willard F. Harley, which has been popularised by other authors and preachers. The concept of love banks works similarly to the principles of banking - traditionally, we are allowed to make deposits and withdrawals from a bank account. Likewise, we can make deposits and withdrawals from the love account we hold with a person of interest. There are four key principles of managing the love account

1. When we associate good feelings with someone, they make a deposit in the love account
2. When you associate bad feelings with someone, they make withdrawals from the love account
3. When it falls below a threshold (overdrawn), you will lose that feeling of love for that person. If we make more withdrawals than deposits, our accounts will be zero
4. If the account reaches a certain level of deposits (the romantic love threshold), the feeling of love is triggered.

Although the concept was predominately geared toward married couples, I believe it applies to all regardless of whether or not you are planning a romantic relationship. Everyone we know has an account and the things they do either deposit or withdraw love units from their accounts. The love bank keeps track of the way each person treats us. Many people have suffered heartbreak because they have given something valuable to someone who does not value it or comprehend how valuable it is. Christians often find themselves in relationships they know they should not be involved in because the person they are interested in has managed to deposit a love unit into their love account, which has reached a romantic threshold. The old friend from Margaret Feinberg's story could have acted unscrupulously by stringing her along in a relationship, which had no future. He would keep giving her nonsensical excuses why he hadn't taken the next step. Our emotions give us the feeling of falling in love. When we identify someone who makes us happy, we are also motivated to reciprocate by making that person happy. There are serious consequences in toying with human emotions. The Scripture tells us, "Hope deferred makes the heart sick…" (Proverbs 13:12). It is crucial to keep our communication lines open with the other person so that hopes and expectations are well managed.

## REFLECTION QUESTIONS

1. Who are you? How would you describe yourself?
2. Where are you going with your life? Where do you see yourself in five years? What is your biggest dream?
3. What are your strengths? What do you bring to the table in a relationship?
4. What are your weaknesses? What things do you need to work on? What aspect of the fruit of the spirit are you yet to develop?

5. What are your biggest accomplishments?
6. What are your biggest failures?
7. What love language(s) do you speak?
8. What is your motive for getting married?

## PRAYER POINTS

1. Father, thank You for You alone are the perfect matchmaker
2. Father, reveal my true identity to me in Jesus' name
3. Father, please reveal Your purpose for my life to me
4. Father, by the power of Your Holy Spirit, please direct me in areas of friendship, relationship, ministry, employment, career, and finances
5. Father, help me to love You with all my heart, soul, strength, and mind

# CHAPTER 2

## I Think I'm Falling in Love?

### DEFINING LOVE

Love is a dream; marriage is an alarm clock. Most young adults see marriage as their ticket to happiness and fulfilment, but when they get in it, they find themselves unprepared. Love is the foundation of any relationship. There must have been an element of love in a relationship before the couple decided to proceed to the altar to be solemnised. When a couple decides to separate, you might ask what happened to the love they once had for one another? One of the reasons for separation is an inadequate definition of love. Most people define love based on their age, status, educational background, etc. If you ask a teenage girl, what is love? Her answer will be quite different from a fifty-year-old woman who is seeking stability and commitment from her husband. If I ask you what love is, how would you define it? A feeling or emotion? Spirituality? Physical attractiveness? Each answer appeals to different aspects of our triune nature. Man is defined in the scripture as a spirit with a soul and dwells in a body (see 1 Thessalonians 5:23).

Love is three dimensional in nature just as man is triune in nature. It is not purely physical; neither is it purely emotional or spiritual. Each aspect of man gives a different definition of love. When you find someone physically attractive, your body is responsible for the definition of love at that moment. Some ladies can sit in a room listening to a brilliant professor, who is much older than they are, speak for hours. However, they don't find him physically attractive but find him intellectually stimulating. Their soul is giving them a definition of love. You might like your local church Pastor not because you find him physically attractive, but you are attracted to the prestige of the office he holds, and the spiritual authority he possesses.

I shared the story of a couple, James and Jane, in chapter one. They were both physically attracted to each other, which led to them getting married. However, the physical attraction did not translate into mental stimulation for Jane. She wanted intellectual discussions with her husband, which he could not fulfil; hence they were getting a divorce. By no means am I suggesting that people from two different professional training cannot marry each other.

The challenge is finding someone suitable for you. In other words, you find them physically attractive and feel comfortable sharing your thoughts, ideas, dreams, and aspirations with. Also, you trust that they won't lead you astray from the path of righteousness that leads to life.

I have been privy to the testimony of a young man and a lady who were about to get married. They loved each other very much. The young man was inclined to go into the service of God but was yet to be ordained. During their premarital counselling, there was discussion about compatibility. They are were physically attracted to each other, mentally stimulated by each other, but the lady had no interest in ministry. If they ignored this aspect of their love, the marriage would not have lasted. Due to the difference in vision and aspiration, they separated—no one aspect of our triune nature can be classified as more important than the other when it comes to love. One of the reasons for extra-marital affairs is when there is no fulfilment in one of the aspects of our triune being, so we naturally seek for it elsewhere.

Great marriages are built on correct marital education. Most adults in their early twenties are still developing their beliefs and values, which means they are still discovering who they are. There are myths about falling in love and being in relationships that have driven many young adults into the arms of the wrong person. They think that when they fall in love, the person they are in love with will sweep them off their feet and deliver them from all of life's challenges. It is a misleading myth, setting people up for failure and disappointment. Paul's definition of love in 1st Corinthians 13 is quite different from how the world defines it. Love is kind, gentle, considerate, which means the person you are with always considers how their decisions or actions will affect you before making it. They think carefully about their words and how it affects your feelings, whether or not you'd feel comfortable with what they have said or asked you to do. They consider what you think about the choices they are making so that their actions do not destroy your future. No one likes someone who does not have a check on their emotions or the maturity to manage the challenges of life; they are jealous or angry even when there is no cause for it. Now you might begin to see the importance of the fruit of the Spirit. God works in ways that will enable us to control our anger and for ways to help us overcome jealousy and become more forgiving.

Contrary to what you might think, exhibiting love doesn't come naturally to us. Selfishness does, and it will eventually show itself in the relationship; the Adamic nature is ever-present. Don't let the chemistry of the moment with your partner fool you. The chemistry between couples will hide faults for a moment, but it is only going to be for a moment. If we are selfish individuals before we fall in love, we are going to be selfish individuals after we fall in love.

## LOVE MYTHS - ALL I NEED IS LOVE

If love were all we needed for success in relationship, then every one of us would have married the first man or woman we fell in love with. When two people start dating, and they become sexually active with each other, the world says, "as long as they are in love, what difference does it make whether or not they have a piece of paper that states that they are married?" Sometimes to justify their position, they add a few bible verses like God is love, Jesus says, we should not judge, or love thy neighbour as thyself. What we end up with is something that sounds good but is not biblical. We are going to examine common love myths. There are four different words used to express love that broadens our understanding of what love is:

1.  Eros Love from which we get the word erotic. It is associated with physical or sensual love.
2.  Storge Love. This is a familial type of love. It is associated with family ties or relationships. Love for a brother or sister, a dad, or a son.
3.  Philo Love. This word is often translated as friendship or brotherly Love and is social in nature. We can reference the friendship of David and Jonathan.
4.  Agape Love. This is God's kind of love. "For God so loved the world...." (John 3:16). What Jesus Christ did on the cross of Calvary best describes agape love. It is a unconditional commitment to an imperfect person.

**Love Myths #1:**
*Having sex is no big deal. Everybody's doing it.*

The truth is sex is a big deal and an important topic that is very difficult to discuss. It can be uncomfortable and embarrassing. Most churches are silent about it; all they do is tell people don't do it, which is not enough to dissuade young unmarried adults in relationships. Because everyone is doing it, doesn't make it right. The Scriptures tell us of the Hebrew boys, who chose not to defile themselves with the kings' portion of food (see Daniel 1:8-16). Rushing into sex with a person you are not married to causes hormones to rage and often clouds your judgment of the person. It leads to a relationship built on lust instead of love. Sex outside marriage masks the real problem in the relationship; you are never forced to look deeply at underlying issues. You often find that you cannot have any real conversations about the direction you both want the relationship to move in. This affects women more than it does men. If the relationship ends without hopes of marriage being fulfilled, it makes the parties involved feel used and somewhat scarred. The man may feel like a victor, while the lady feels like the victim. The world looks at a man that has sex with a lot of women as a stud, but at a woman that has sex with a lot of men as a whore.

Love is not sex. If sex equates to love, then prostitutes would give the most amount of love. The world profits significantly from the use of sex as a tool, especially in commercials. It's challenging to find a product in the market today without sexual innuendos. Sometimes, you might wonder, are they selling coffee or sex? The picture of sex that our culture paints are a cheap counterfeit of God's design. What they have done is desensitised us by taking something sacred and holy and made it dirty. The sexual life of the unmarried person is of great importance to God. There is no single act that reflects the idea of becoming one flesh more than sex. Hence, it is more than just a physical act. The grass always looks greener on the other side; don't jump the fence only to get disappointed. The intimacy that avoids commitment will leave us broken and lonelier than ever. Sex outside marriage never delivers on its promises, and instant gratification does not produce long term happiness.

Sex should not be view as a currency or a medium of exchange. You don't owe your partner sex because he takes you out to dinner, buys you a gift, or says, "I love you." It is unfair for anyone to claim that you don't love them because you refuse to go to bed with them. Your past mistakes should not be used as a yardstick for your future actions; no one has the right to pressure you into doing something you are not comfortable with, especially when it goes against your faith and beliefs.

## Love Myths #2:
### *Don't buy it, till you try it*

Unmarried couples use various rationales to justify sex outside marriage, such as "It's okay if you're in love," "Everybody's doing it," "We need to sleep together before we get married so we can know if we are sexually compatible." I had a lady approach me with a logical argument on the subject; she said to me, "Do you buy clothes in the shop without trying it on?" To which I replied, "No, we have changing rooms in most shops to see how it fits." Then she responded, "How do you expect me to marry a man without knowing whether or not he is good in bed?" This sounds perfectly logical.  In other words, "Don't buy it, till you try it." A piece of clothing can be taken back to the store after a few days, provided you have your receipt. Your virginity is something that you can only give away once! When it is gone, it cannot be replaced, and you lose a precious part of you that should have been reserved for your bride or your groom.

Pastor Todd Bishop shared a Testimony in his sermon on sex, about a Lady by the name of Ellen Petrakis. This is her testimony; I was about 14 years old, just starting high school when I decided to save myself for marriage. Having grown up in church, I knew that it was the right thing to do. I felt very strongly about waiting for my husband, and even though all of my friends felt differently, they always respected my decision. Even my guy friends respected how I felt; however, they always tried to get me to change my mind! As the years went by, I watched as my friends dated guys, slept with them, and then broke up.

I remember listening to my friend Pam as she cried her eyes out when she found out she was diagnosed with HPV, an incurable STD she got from a guy she hardly knew. I begged my best friend not to go through with her abortion when she got pregnant, but she refused my help. I remember looking into my friend Rebecca's eyes as she lay on a hospital bed at South Oaks, recovering from her suicide attempt. She tried to kill herself because after she gave her virginity to her boyfriend, he broke up with her for another girl. It confirmed to me that I had made the right decision. These guys didn't care for these girls; mostly, they just used them. It became "known" that I was a virgin and wasn't one of those girls. It made me different from everyone else, and when people asked me why, I could tell them about my relationship with God and how he wants us to wait until marriage and how I wanted to do that for him.
I would tell myself that until a guy is willing to get up in front of my family, his family, and God, and promise to love me forever, he didn't deserve me. It was that simple. My mom always told me that I would be the one the guys would remember, not the ten other girls he slept with. He would remember me because I wouldn't sleep with him! And I can tell you today that my mother was right. Years later, when I ran into old boyfriends or even just my guy friends, they would always say, "there was something different about you – you weren't like the other girls." They may not have known it at

the time, but in a way, they respected me and realised why later on. Well, high school came and went. I had boyfriends, some waited, and respected my decision, and some didn't. College came and went, more boyfriends - some waited, some didn't. When I turned 25, I realised I had dated all these guys, and not one was worthy, not one was the one that God had for me. I was so thankful that even though I may have wasted some time and went through a lot of heartaches, I was faithful to God and did not give away my virginity. I was still waiting to give that gift to my husband. I promised God I would stop dating and just wait. Wait for the one He had for me. Well, about a year and a half went by, and I was still waiting. Now I was starting to get worried! Here I am a 26-year-old virgin! Did I really wait all these years and now I'm still waiting? My patience was running out. I had read so many books on how to be single – I just couldn't read one more book! I would joke around with God and say when is he going to walk through those church doors? I can't wait anymore!

Well, it was Sunday, July 11th, 2004, when this gorgeous guy comes walking through the church doors. As soon as I saw him, I fell in love. The moment we met, I just knew that he was the one. God had promised me that He would confirm it to me, and He did. The very first time we hung out, it was amazing. All the questions, all the doubts they just went away. I looked into the eyes of this man, and I could say I waited for you! You're the one! And to know that God was in it, that He had planned for this day to happen was incredible.

I can tell you it is so amazing to give this gift to your husband. You loved him so much before you even knew him to save yourself just for him. I have some pictures to show you from our wedding that took place this summer. We were married on July 7th, almost exactly two years after we met in the Bahamas. Pastor Todd married us, and this is the day that I waited for.

This testimony proves that the myth of "don't buy it, till you try it" is just that precisely, "a myth." I know of countless young men and women who have bought into this lie and have given themselves to someone who did not end up becoming their spouse. Remember, Love is Patient.

## Love Myths #3:
### *There are no consequences of premarital sex*

The consequences of premarital sex are real; it includes unwanted pregnancy, abortion, guilt, shame, emotional emptiness, sexually transmitted diseases, and spiritual bondage. Our Government has tried to reduce the number of teenage pregnancies by introducing sex education and contraceptive, but they have failed to find a device to protect a person's heart. When the heart is assaulted, defensive patterns are developed that will affect any future relationship. As we bond and break, over and over again, we lose our ability to bond properly. We may lose faith in falling in love ever again.

Having multiple sexual partners opens the door for ungodly comparison. It might lead to unrealistic expectations in the marital bed, and sometimes resentment that may never heal. Your spouse might ask you, "What did you keep for me? If every scared act has been done with someone else." Perhaps the most significant consequences of premarital sex are spiritual. The physical act translates to a spiritual bond, which creates an unhealthy soul tie. It gives access to strange personalities to wreak havoc in their victim's lives. If, after you have left a relationship, you find yourself thinking about the person obsessively, you can't get them out of your mind; it is an indication that there is a soul tie in place.

"Do you not know that he who unites himself with a prostitute is one with her in the body? For it is said, "The two will become one flesh." (1 Corinthians 6:16)

There are spiritual entities known as spirit wife and spirit husband; they are, in many cases, responsible for marital delays in the lives of their victim. I'm privy to the testimony of a young man who dated a lady he thought he was going to marry. They were both in love and engaging in sexual intercourse regularly. Eventually, they broke up their engagement, and they went their separate ways. What looks broken on the surface, was firmly intact spiritually. The young man told me; he had a dream in which he saw himself marrying the lady; this means they were legally married spiritually. That prevented him from being able to marry someone else physically. It took him eight years of praying and deliverance to break the bond spiritually. Just as physical divorce isn't cordial, spiritual separation isn't amiable too. Getting into it is easy; getting out of it is more complicated. A spirit wife and spirit husband has a legal right in the lives of their victims, just as a man or woman has the right to his or her spouse's property. And they won't surrender very easily. The smartest way to outsmart the devil is to obey God.

## Love Myths #4:
### *Waiting for Mr. or Ms. Right*

The myth goes something like this, "somewhere out there is the right person for me. I will know when I find the person because there will be an instant connection between us, undeniable chemistry. "The truth is, finding the right man or woman is not going to change you into a better person. If you are a lazy person before a relationship, finding a hard-working person is not going to transform you overnight into a hard-working person. Or, if you are a self-centred person before a relationship, finding a generous person is not going to change who you are. The myth makes us think that if we get the right person in our life, then we'll be happy. This false assumption makes us think, "I don't have to change anything about myself; he or she wouldn't have to change anything about themselves, we will be made for each other, and everything is going to be perfect." If you take a moment to ask anyone who has been married for any period, they will tell you that change is one permanent factor of marriage. None of us is married to a perfect person; we have all changed and evolved over the years in our relationship.

The most important thing is to become Mr. or Ms. Right yourself. Learn to evaluate yourself according to the standard you are demanding from others. Some young men have missed out on lovely young ladies because they have set their sight on the pictures of models in magazines, which has been edited or photoshopped. Some people are not comfortable in their skin; my advice is don't try to be something you are not - if you are a size 8 be happy being a size 8, if you are a size 16 be satisfied being a size 16. Some men like a woman with a little meat on her bones, "you are fearfully and wonderfully made…" (Psalm 139:14). It is important to accept yourself for who you are, but don't use that as an excuse to let yourself go but, also, don't try to live up to some sort of super-model expectation. Couples want to be proud of their partner's appearance, not embarrassed. Small changes can make a world of difference in your appearance as well as your outlook.

Your relationship with the Lord will influence your world view; a lot of people call themselves Christian because they go to church. If the person you are interested in is not Christ-centric, you will find yourself very alone in one of the most important realms of life, your spiritual life. Here are some qualities to look for in a healthy relationship; do they have a prayer life? Do they make the word of God their priority? Do they study the word of God deeper than just the Sunday sermon? Do they belong to a small group of people who are continually mining the word of God? Do they serve in some capacity in their local church? An objection to my questions is to say, "I am not marrying a Pastor or Preacher, why do I need to ask these questions?" The scripture makes us understand, "When the foundations are being destroyed, what can the righteous do?" (Psalms 11:3). If you fail in getting your foundation right, you might spend a lifetime trying to fix it, instead of making progress with your destiny. You cannot cut corners when it comes to the foundation of your future. I am not saying that there aren't some good people out there who are not Christians, but the bible makes us understand, "Do not be yoked together with unbelievers" (2 Corinthians 6:14).

## Love Myths #5:
### *Love is money, I want a rich partner who can take care of me*

Many young adults dream of what it would be like being rich, flying first class, having expensive holidays, living the life of a celebrity, etc. But valuing money over good character may seem superficial. When we marry for money, it is like having a job you don't like, but you still do it because of the benefits. You might decide to quit when the going gets tough, or when hard times come. You don't want to feel or be called a gold digger, so we shouldn't marry for money or exploit our partner to enrich ourselves. Money doesn't readily translate into happiness; wealthier couples don't necessarily last longer than those who earn less. I would be the first to tell you that money is an essential aspect of marriage. To underestimate the importance of money in a relationship is to be naïve, financial security is a significant factor in choosing to get married. Money is among the top reasons why many marriages fail; it gives a lot of freedom and options to do what you want to do, when you want to do it, enabling you to live the life of your dreams. While money can ease the financial pressure in a relationship, it does not make up for everything.

Money shifts the balance of power in the relationship; partners sometimes can turn to financial bullying when they hold all the money cards. Your ideas and opinions are not valued because they believe you are not going to make any financial contributions (see Ecclesiastes 9:16). On many occasions, you might feel compelled to give in to their demands at your personal expense. "If you love me, you will sleep with me." Don't mistake sex for love; Cinderella didn't lose her virginity to find and keep prince charming, she lost her slipper. You don't need to have sex to keep your prince. Remember, the golden rule is, "he that has the gold makes the rules." Life is too short for you to settle for someone who will mistreat you. Men with high net worth often like a trophy wife, if you think your beauty might be your way into a particular social class; with time, beauty does fade. Marriages that cross different social class boundaries may not present a distinct set of challenges initially. With time you might begin to feel like a fish out of water, because you are moving outside your comfort zone, into the uncharted territory in this new social class. You must be willing to learn very quickly about things like etiquette, topics for conversation, the dos and don'ts, etc.

Sometimes a wealthy partner will demand a pre-nuptial agreement to safeguard their assets; this is not uncommon in the 21st Century. It means that in the event of a failure in the marriage, you might be limited to the assets you take away from them. People who watched their parents struggle through life don't want the same for themselves. If we're going to pledge our lives to someone, why not have it be a financially secured one. I dated a lady some years before I got married, whose mother didn't like me because I was inclined to be a man of God. Her reasoning was, I was not going to be financially secure and be able to look after her daughter. She often made a jest of my belief. Parents want security for their children. I quickly learnt money matters in matrimony as much as love does. Putting money ahead of love is like trying to fly before you have learnt to work.

## THE FRANKENSTEIN THEORY

Love is a decision you have to make every day. The truth is, you will always find someone who is more beautiful, more eloquent, more charming, and more intelligent than your partner. However, it doesn't give us the right to break up with our partner each time we find someone we think is better. Love is a decision that you make every morning you wake up; you have to make the decision that I will love you no matter what. There is a classic horror novel called Frankenstein by Mary Shelley. In her book, she tells the story of a young scientist who creates a human monster from a scientific experiment. He used various parts of different dead people to form the ultimate human being. What many people want in their potential spouse is nothing more than a Frankenstein Monster. They want different parts from different people amalgamated into a single entity. We want a partner who has the legs of Mary, the hands of Rachel, the face of Hannah and has the character of Elizabeth.

The truth is, I was one of those who was chasing after the Frankenstein Monster. At the age of 26, I sat down one night, and I wrote 44 points describing the ideal lady I wanted to marry. Looking back now, I was really naïve and immature. The list I wrote consisted of mostly physical attributes. My definition of love at that time in my life was incomplete and void of understanding. It is imperative to identify our deepest needs, admittedly, this can be a scary prospect, but if you don't, we will never see ourselves with any clarity. Everyone will always be the wrong partner.

Being able to see the potential in your partner is far more important than the glitz and glamour we perceive as beauty. Not all that glitters is gold. Most people are familiar with the Pareto Principle, often referred to as the 80/20 rule. The theory centres on the idea that no one person can meet 100% of your needs all the time. In other words, do not leave a partner who has 80% of what you need, for a person who has 20% of what you want. Many adults have destroyed their marriages when they fail to adhere to this principle. They have chased after the 20% and lost the 80%.

Don't panic if you find yourself in a situation where someone you consider a priority considers you optional; it just means you have not met the one. There is a parable of the long spoon. The author is unknown, but the parable is credited to Rabbi Haim of Romshishok. In this parable, there are two groups of hungry people who sat at a table with a lot of food to eat, but they were forced to use long spoons to reach the food that is right there in front of them. One group was focused on feeding themselves, each time they tried, they failed, and so they continued to starve. The other group quickly realize that it was impossible to feed themselves with the long spoon, so they decided to feed each other. In so doing, each person uses their spoon to feed someone else at the table. Relationships are based on giving and receiving. It doesn't work if it consists of only giving and not receiving. Having the right balance is critical.

## REFLECTIONS QUESTIONS

These are very practical questions you can ask of someone fairly early on in a relationship in a non-threatening way and get an honest picture of their character

1. What is love? (How would you define love?)
2. What are the common mistakes people make when it comes to love?
3. What changes would you make to your definition of love?
4. What do you seek in a partner? Are they committed to church? Are they caring or charming? Are they actively involved in a small group? Do they spend time daily in the Word, growing in their faith?
5. Are you waiting for Mr. or Ms. Right?

# PRAYER POINTS

1. Father, thank you for loving me, unconditionally.
2. Father, please heal me of broken hearts and wounded spirits in Jesus' name
3. Father, Please forgive me for not trusting and yielding to the temptation of the flesh
4. Every transference of evil into my life through sexual intercourse be destroyed by the fire of the Holy Spirit
5. Every evil seed planted through my sexual intercourse be uprooted
6. Father expose men or women who are wolves in sheep's clothing to me in Jesus' name
7. Father grant me the grace to be faithful in my service to you, help me to seek and thirst after righteousness in Jesus' name

# CHAPTER 3

# Cycles of a Relationship

In this chapter, I have adapted the work of Dr. Bruce Tuckman to help with the understanding of the stages we go through in a relationship. Dr. Bruce proposed that every team goes through four stages of development, which are Forming, Storming, Norming, and Performing. A relationship, in essence, is two individuals coming together to form a team. The scripture consistently emphasises the importance of teamwork, "Two are better than one because they have a good return for their labour," (Ecclesiastes 4:9) Jesus though being the son of the living God, needed the 12 disciples. We all have individual talents or gifts, but we still need each other.

How well a team performs is determined by how quickly they get through each phase of their relationship. You can't expect a new team to perform well the first time they come together. Individually, each member of a team might be brilliant but lacks what makes the team perform well. Likewise, in a romantic relationship, a couple often might be wonderful people individually but cannot get along with others. The most natural approach is to blame someone else. As we work through these phases, it helps couples to minimise the conflicts and heartbreak that come from each of the stages.

## PHASE 1: FORMING

*"Can two walk together, except they be agreed?"* (Amos 3:3)

Congratulations, she said yes to a date. The early stage of a relationship is marked by intense attraction and infatuation. At this stage of the relationship, you appear to be 'over the moon' about your new partner. The excitement will probably last a few weeks or months, depending on various factors, such as the proximity of the couple to each other, frequency of your dates, age, and of course, maturity. I have seen young adults deciding to commit the rest of their lives to each other at this stage of their relationship. It would be premature, and in many cases, the decision doesn't last. We should not make a permanent decision on inadequate information. This stage is ideal for asking fundamental questions, such as where the relationship is heading, your partners' values, their vision, their influences, religious beliefs, etc. Most people are not defensive of the truth at this stage, but I am not recommending that this should be the topic of your conversation on the first date.

Think of the date as a job interview. Every job vacancy has a description and responsibilities attached to it. When a man asks a lady on a date, he is putting himself forward as an ideal candidate for a role. By default, he acknowledges that he understands the duties and responsibilities attached to the position. Also, he has the skillset or competency to fulfil the role. He should not feel awkward or unprepared if the lady asks him; why do you want to be in a relationship with me? Or, where do you see yourself in five years? If his answer is along the lines, "I like the way you look," then he probably hasn't thought deeply enough about the role. If a lady accepts an invite for a date, she thinks of the man as a potentially suitable candidate for the role. If she rejects the invite for a date, then she thinks the man is not a suitable candidate. After all, it is not every job you apply for; you get a call for an interview. Some jobs go through multiple levels of screening. I have been for a job interview where I went through three rounds of screening with a different part of the business each time; my point is that it might take more than one date before you can decide, so hang in there. The process can be gruelling. It takes work to find a gem. The scriptures tell us, "He who finds a wife finds a good thing and obtains favour from the Lord." (Proverbs 18:22)

No one in their right mind would allow an unqualified doctor to perform surgery on them. We often take great pride in our academic achievements, especially when we have graduated top of our class from a prestigious school, such as Harvard, Cambridge, etc. We can present our certificate with confidence to our prospective employer, indicating why we are the most qualified candidate for the role. Many Christians walk to the altar with people not qualified for the role of a husband or a wife. They ignore God in the process of selecting a spouse but want his blessing on their wedding day so that they can live happily ever after. God is interested in every aspect of our life, including the choice of a wife or husband. He saw Adam alone in the garden, and He said, "It is not good for a man to be alone. I will make a helper suitable for him."(Genesis 2:18) He understands that we can be lonely at times, and in a hurry, but He knows that it is better for us to be single than to be in a bad relationship or marriage that kills your destiny.

Before you move to the next phase in your relationship with your partner, it is crucial to do some due diligence by getting Godly counsel from the people around you, beginning with your parents. Parents often seem to be out of date to their children, especially in the area of relationships. Good parents pass down the wisdom for a successful relationship and marriage to their children. I am a testimony of that; my mother was key in my marital decision. The bible tells us to honour our parents in all things, including the choice of a spouse (see Ephesians 6:2). I hope we don't end up like Esau, who married a wife who was a source of grief to his parents, and as a result, he missed out on his parent's blessings (see Genesis 26:34-35). Mothers especially have a sixth sense, an eye for the invisible, they can smell fraud and a liar from afar. I have stories of young adults who missed their step in life when they refused parental counsel in marriage. They live with regret until today.

Another crucial screening is from spiritual parents and mentors. My assumption is, you belong to a household of faith, or you are under a spiritual covering. A Pastor provides a spiritual oversight over your marital journey, and mentors stir you in the right direction. My mentors have been instrumental in my marital journey.

They counselled my wife and me before we got married about the journey of marriage, what to expect, and pitfalls to avoid. Late Archbishop Benson Idahosa made a statement, "you should take advice from a man who has gone the journey twice, which you are trying to take once." Experiences of my mentors are invaluable to me; I appreciate their influence in my life very much.

Finally, Godly witnesses. Before you commit to your new partner, take the time to find out their reputation from other people. The scriptures tell us, "In the mouth of two or three witnesses, the truth shall be established." (2 Corinthians 13:1) What kind of testimony do you have with people? What adjectives would people use to define you if you were not present? I tell young adults, someone somewhere is taking note. David was a shepherd boy who spent his days in the wilderness, looking after his father's sheep. One day someone recommended him for a job in the palace. The bible did not record who recommended him (see 1 Samuel 16:14-19). Someone took note of his skills as a musician, though he was just a shepherd boy. Take for example, if I mentioned the name Judas, do you immediately think about the disciple who betrayed Jesus? What is your name synonymous with? Because that is your reputation. I hope you have a good one. Take care of your character, and your reputation will take care of itself.

## PHASE 2: STORMING

*"In your anger do not sin; do not let the sun go down while you are still angry."* (Ephesians 4:26)

How long a relationship lasts is determined by how well the couple can manage their differences. Every relationship comes with its challenges. Most young couples are not equipped with their tools to resolve conflicts amicably. The most common tool in the toolbox is the silent treatment, verbal assault, physical assault, sarcasm, angry outburst, shouting match, sweeping the issue under the carpet, or quit the relationship. It makes the storming stage the most challenging phase in a relationship. If care is not taken, the storming stage is where the relationship ends. A typical question asked is how long does each step of the cycle lasts. There's no accurate scientific answer to that question; most people move from one stage of the cycle to the next at their own pace. The key is to recognise which phase you are in with your partner and work together with them to move successfully from one stage to the next. The temptation is to quit the relationship when you get into the storming phase of the relationship. My advice is counting the cost of stopping and restarting all over again. The truth is, if you quit a relationship today, and meet somebody new tomorrow, you have to start the whole process from the beginning again and still go through another storming phase. We only trade one set of problems for another.

Anyone who has been in a romantic relationship knows that disagreement is inevitable. When two people with different backgrounds come together to form a team, they come along with their baggage, which includes, habits, personalities, experiences, expectations, traditions, and their general way of doing things. What may seem reasonable to you might be utterly alien to the other person. We are all wired differently. I made mention in the previous chapter that there are myths about the love of meeting Mr. or Ms. Right isn't true. The more you spend time with your partner, the more you will start to notice your differences. You may feel your partner is too social, but he may see you as a hermit. After one hour at a party, you want to leave; he's just getting into the music. Much irritation can be avoided by merely understanding the differences between you and your partner. If you manage disagreements well, they can become opportunities for you and your partner to align your values, learn about each other, evaluate your moral stands on a critical issue and deepen your love for one another.

Effective communication is critical when resolving a conflict, and everyone deserves to be treated with respect, even if their opinion is nonsensical to you. A crucial part of effective communication is listening (see James 1:19); many of us are listening to respond and not listening to understand. As a general rule, avoid being a historian when there is a disagreement - don't bring out the mental notebook of events and memories of every past argument, the date, the time, the location, and the reasons. The reason for this is simple, the current conflict is not dealt with, and the person feels attacked. In the heat of an argument, we usually only see one side, which is our own. If we calm down, we can almost always begin to see the issue from the other person's point of view. Repetitive conflict tells us there is an underlying issue that is yet to be addressed.

"Do not be quickly provoked in your spirit, for anger resides in the lap of fools." (Ecclesiastes 7:9)

The storming stage doesn't indicate incompatibility between the couple. But in some extreme cases, it does suggest that the relationship shouldn't proceed into the engagement stage. During an argument, if the lady feels physically threatened by her partner, this should serve as a red flag that needs to be addressed and not swept under the carpet. I recommend that you seek Godly counsel from a spiritual parent or trusted marital counsellor (see Proverbs 11:14). If the couple has a mismatched temperament like one partner having a black belt in verbal karate, he or she might end up being a bully and may use anger as a tool for manipulation to get their way. It can be the man or the woman. They may be a physical bully, a verbal bully, a financial bully, or a psychological bully. They want to have their way.

## PHASE 3: NORMING

The norming stage is the calm after the storm, where the dust settles. At this stage in the relationship, the couple gets into a rhythm with each other. They have a better understanding of their partner and establish some boundaries which are agreed verbally or assumed. It is the point in the relationship where you have to choose whether or not you want to continue to be a couple or go your separate ways. Do not decide out of pity or with the hope that things will get better once you are married. You must set a high standard for the relationship, don't tolerate bad behaviour with the hope that things will get better; the truth and reality are that it won't. Once you have discovered each other's temperament or maturity, they are facts, not assumptions.

With the initial euphoria cleared, there is a tendency for complacency in this stage. You might recall the principle of the love account, stated in an earlier chapter in the book. After the storming stage, the balance of the love account will be depleted; you might recall that you associate the good feelings and pleasant memories with deposits into the account and bad feelings as withdrawals. After each disagreement in the relationship, the love account will be depleted, by how much, I couldn't tell you; there are various factors to determine that. For example, the nature of the conflict, the words that were exchanged, was the issue resolved or swept under the carpet. The couple has to make a conscious effort to check and replenish their love account. The danger is to assume that your love account is still in the black when you're overdrawn. The relationship might end abruptly without one of the parties seeing it coming.

Couples at the norming stage must learn to resolve their differences amicably; it is too simplistic an interpretation that your partner is the wrong one. We tend to point the finger at the person in front of us. A great sign of Maturity is the ability to restrain from blaming others for our unhappiness, insecurities, or mood swing.

You should learn to appreciate your partner's strengths and respect their opinion even if you don't agree with it. You must resist the impulse to respond negatively to any provocation, no matter how personally satisfying it might feel at that moment. Your partner is not your verbal punching bag. As couples continually evolve to fit every changing circumstance in their relationship, they must remind themselves to do the little things that bring joy to their hearts. It could be something as simple as a text message during the day that tells your partner you are thinking of them.

I am privy to the story of a lady who went for counselling a few weeks before her wedding. She walked into the Pastor's office, looking very upset. The Pastor thought it would be a good idea to cheer her up by asking about the wedding plans and if she had managed to get the perfect wedding dress. After all, most ladies dream of their wedding day. Instead of smiling, she broke down in tears. When she finally gathered herself, the words that came out of her mouth were, "I don't want to go through with this anymore." While it is not uncommon in some cases, people do develop cold feet before their big day. She was adamant; she was not going through with the wedding. The Pastor asked a simple question, "Why?" She proceeded to explain that she was lost as a person with her fiancé. She didn't know who she was anymore; she had no voice and personality. Her fiancé always wanted to control her, decide for her, and tell her what she must do. It suddenly dawned on her that she was going to be living the rest of her life with this man. She felt she was living inside someone else's dream.

We all yearn for perfection in our relationship, but we are imperfect human beings. If couples get complacent with each other, the relationship begins to either stagnate or regress. If one of the parties uses anger as a tool for manipulation, the other party is forced to suppress their emotions because they don't want to upset the rhythm of the relationship, especially when the long term goal of the relationship is marriage. Although there are no guarantees, there are characteristics that are generally considered acceptable; the willingness to overlook the flaws of your partner, sensitivity to his or her emotions, ability to express care when needed. On the other hand, characteristics, such as lying, overreacting at the slightest provocation, contempt, proneness to anger, the propensity to harbour a grudge, aggression, an attempt to invalidate a partner's opinion are all considered harmful. However, couples must develop a commitment to growing together and understanding each other's needs and wants, keeping in their minds aimed at the long-term goal of the relationship and its vision.

# PHASE 4: PERFORMING STAGE

*"Where there is no vision, the people perish…"* (Proverbs 29:18)

I would begin by saying that not every couple reaches the performing stage in their relationship. The reason is simple; the couple becomes complacent with each other. They have a routine with their partner, and they are happy with the way things are going. They don't want to upset the balance of their chemistry with their partner. They might even consider moving in together (cohabiting), which is a sin according to God's standard. You might have heard phrases such as "if it isn't' broke, don't fix it." It is quite possible to skip the performing stage and move to engagement, but they run the risk of having an unanswered question knocking at their door for answers sooner rather than later.

What characterises the performing stage is a clearly defined vision and consistent effort made toward the fulfilment of the vision. Adam had a vision and responsibilities before God thought it right to give him a suitable helpmate (see Genesis 2:18). It is vital to take note of the words "suitable helpmate" because not all partners fall into this category. The man casts the vision, and the woman must be able to see herself in the man's vision, although the traditional roles of men and women are quickly changing in the 21st century. However, it doesn't negate the word of God that the man is the head of the home. It's impossible to know if you're successful if you don't see what you're trying to accomplish in the first place. Hence clarity of vision is vital. With today's technology, black and white television are obsolete, so, when we define our vision, it should be in high definition so that you can both see where you're going together (see Habakkuk 2: 2-3).

A visionless relationship goes stale with mundane routines. Dating without a purpose always leave one party feeling short-changed. I know of a couple who dated for six years, but in the end, they went their separate ways. The cost of the six years wasted; I don't think any of us could quantify it. Couples without a vision are vulnerable to negative influence, including the temptation to fornicate or infidelity.

Having a clear vision also removes the tendency for two visions, which causes division and contention. The energy derived from passion is enormous when the couples see each other as complements instead of substitutes. The scriptures tell that nothing is impossible if accomplished when we speak with one voice (see Genesis 11:6). Vision affects every aspect of our life, including how we spend money. If a couple has the vision to marry, then they might consider having a saving pot for the wedding day expenses, they might even sacrifice going out for dinner for this purpose.

As a man, do not feel threatened when your vision is questioned for clarity. We have heard that marriage is a marathon. If a lady asks her partner, "Where are we going to live?" this is not because she is a gold digger, she is merely asking for clarity. For example, the couple lives in different cities; the assumption is that the lady is required to move to where her partner lives when they get married. But in some cases, this might not be the best option. I made mention earlier that the roles of men and women are fast changing in the 21st century. If the woman is earning a six-figure salary, and the man is earning less, how does that impact the decision to move or not to move out of the city? Or she lives in the ideal city for his chosen profession. A discussion is needed to understand the impact of each option available for the couple. Whoever is required to make the sacrifice must understand their reason for the sacrifice, because their vision can be seen ahead.

I will end this chapter by asking the couples in a relationship to carefully consider where they are in the cycle of their relationship. You might not be in the performing stage of the relationship but can see the potential. Sports scouts have an eye for talents in athletes, and they are able to see the potentials when it is unpolished. You do not need to panic; you must look at your partner now and see the potential in them.

## REFLECTION POINTS

1. What are the reasons for conflicts in the relationship?
2. What stage of the relationship cycle am I in?
3. What is the balance of my love account? Is it depleted?
4. What do I need to do to move to the next phase of the relationship?
5. Are there characteristics in me that are stagnating my relationship?

## PRAYER POINTS

1. Father, help me to understand the stage I am in within my relationship in Jesus' name
2. Father, I disconnect myself from any unfruitful relationship, that is hindering my marital destiny in Jesus' name.
3. Father, Your word says it is not good that I am alone, connect me with my help meet today in Jesus' name

4.  Just like you solved Adam's marital challenges, please solve my marital problems today and connect me with my partner in Jesus' name.
5.  Every evil character that may be hindering my marital breakthrough, I destroy it in Jesus' name.

# CHAPTER 4

# The Money Talk

A young lady took her partner home to meet her parents. After dinner, the father of the lady decided to have a private conversation with his future son-in-law. He asked the young man, "Do you love my daughter?" He replied, "Yes." "Do you want to marry my daughter?" He replied, "Yes." "How do you plan to pay for the wedding?" He replied, "God will provide." "Where do you expect to live with my daughter after you are married?" He replied, "God will provide." "How do you plan to support your family?" He replied, "God will provide." Finally, the lady's father left the room angrily and said to his wife, "This young man thinks I am God, and I am paying for everything." Many young adults live on the credit facility available in the form of 'the bank of Mom and Dad.' However, after the wedding day, that credit facility ceases to exist. The Bible says that "the man will leave his family and cleave to his wife, and they shall become one flesh." (Genesis 2:24) If the financial umbilical cord is not cut off on or before the wedding, a couple may bring unwanted interference into their marriage. Admittedly, "he who pays the piper dictates the tune."

For a couple to understand the "for richer, for poorer" part of their wedding vow, it begins with understanding God's plan for their finances. Most newlyweds have a problem with their finances shortly after their wedding, due to accumulated debt in personal obligations, such as wedding costs, student loans, or credit cards, etc. These financial commitments often take its toll on the marriage quickly. If they don't pay attention to the way money functions within their relationship, then communication and love breaks down. Money talk matters because it allows a couple to manage each other's expectations openly and transparently. Knowing how much money your partner makes is essential, and so they do not become too curious. I'm not saying you have to start asking for their bank statements on a second date, but if you plan to marry, then financial transparency is a must. It dictates not only what they can do with their lives, but what limitations they have as a couple. They must learn to think and plan to avoid problems (see Proverbs 22:3). Too often, couples put off money talk until they are so deeply in debt, and it seems impossible to get out. Then they blame each other for their woes; they are reacting instead of planning.

# THE PRINCIPLE OF WORK

*"The Lord God took the man and put him in the Garden of Eden to work it and take care of it."* (Genesis 2:15)

The concept of work has its origin in God. Adam had a job before God gave him a wife. Work is a priority before marriage; it is a mark of maturity. Financial trouble is one of the top five reasons for divorce. There is dignity in labour. A man without the ability to hold down a job or a clear career path should not be considering marriage as his next step in life. The man is expected to be the provider; hence, he must demonstrate the ability to provide for his family if he plans to start one. My words might sound harsh, but this is reality. The scriptures say, "Anyone who does not provide for their relatives, and especially for their household, has denied the faith and is worse than an unbeliever." (1 Timothy 5:8) We cannot preach faith without work.

The traditional roles of men and women are changing. Women are no longer stay-at-home moms in the 21st Century; they are ambitious and hard-working. It is a good thing and should be celebrated because it provides additional income for the household. However, the couple needs to clarify their career paths. Other than the apparent fact that a career affects income, it also plays a significant role in the family dynamics, like when the couple will have children or how many children they will have. As a student, I worked as a sales representative at my local cinema. I was a maths tutor and also a part-time musician. I did not consider any of these jobs as my career path, as I was in the university pursuing a degree. "Where do you see yourself in five-years with your career path?" This is a question that should be asked and answered between couples. A career path will create the right expectation of the kind of lifestyle they would be living and how to plan for future projects.

It is fine to support your partner in challenging times (job loss, health issues, etc.) and have them do the same for you, but you don't always have to carry them. No one likes a lazy freeloader. There must be a mutual understanding that everyone will take their fair share of responsibilities. Some men admire women who bring more to the table than just a pretty face. And vice-versa, women prefer a man who brings more to the table than his six-pack. I heard a lady once remark, "six-packs' don't pay the bills."

Men have fragile egos contrarily to what many ladies might think. We might be physically big and strong, but our emotions can be bruise just as easily as the lady. We derive self-esteem and confidence from professional success. When the topic of work is discussed, it must be done with care and sensitivity. Some men are intimidated by high achieving women and feel insecure about their accomplishments, so take the time to communicate your needs and listen to your partner's needs. If you find your partner is not committed to their career, it might be a warning sign of what the future holds.

## BUDGETING

*"Which of you, desiring to build a tower, does not first sit down and count the cost, whether he has enough to complete it?"* (Luke 14:28)

Money isn't everything, but it's sure close to breathing. We all have different thoughts and opinions about money. Some people are frugal, while others are extravagant and carefree with their spending. A budget allows the couple to align their financial priorities so that funds are directed where it is needed the most. The aim is not to police your partner's every-spend, but to build mutual trust that your partner makes the right judgements with their finances, especially where you have joint financial forces. Dave Ramsey's book, the 'Total Money Makeover,' states, "Every penny should have a name."

A Budget is a control tool that stops us from being tempted to go beyond our limits. The couple must learn to say "No" to borrowing to buy consumable items that depreciate. Their lifestyle needs to align with their income and not what they wish it were. I do not mean couples should not borrow at all; most couples have to borrow to buy a house. I see that as an investment, the goal is to avoid financial bondage by staying out of additional debt and committing to paying off existing debt. Couples should work together to develop financial plans that match their income and goals.

One of the biggest mistakes couples make in budgeting is allowing their ego to play a part in the decision-making. Society customs governing which spouse manages the family finances are changing. Traditionally, this responsibility falls on the man, a value underscored by the leadership committed to the husband in Scriptures (see Ephesians 5:23). Although the husband is to be the head of the home, wives can contribute significantly to the family economy by applying their financial wisdom and skills. We must understand our weaknesses and strengths. There must be a designated bookkeeper, and this can be the man or the woman. It doesn't always have to be the man. Allow me to share the story of a couple with you. They have been married for some years. The husband was an excellent salesman who averaged about half a million dollars per year. Despite his substantial income, he still manages to be in debt, so they went to see their Pastor for counsel. The Pastor counselled them to change their financial management approach, "let your wife handle the accounts of the family, but you can have a portion of the income to do whatever you wish." The new approach worked like a miracle, and the books were balanced. The family was out of debt within a year. Sometimes the wife has more exceptional financial and budgetary skills, and a wise husband should take note. A wife may be better at maintaining the budget and balancing the accounts of the family - handling the payment of the bills. In such cases, the family may be better off having her handle these responsibilities. The control over money is far more critical than how much we make. Making decisions about buying a house or car, taking a holiday, or even the choice of groceries can become problematic when couples have different opinions on how money should be spent. Much effort goes into planning the details of the wedding day, but less energy is put into preparing for the happily ever after. Budgeting is crucial to the survival of the relationship, especially in a situation where the couple needs to scrimp and save. Couples sometimes come from different social backgrounds. For example, inherited wealth, royalty, or blue-collar workers. What could be considered as the norm in one place will be utterly alien in another. It could be reasonable to have lunch at a restaurant in Tiffany's or to shop at Harrods for Christmas, while it could be wise for you to pick up clothes from a thrift shop.

Living according to a workable budget for the first time can feel practically impossible for new couples. Spending habits are not easy to change, especially in our consumer culture. The message 'buy it now and pay later' is very attractive, we've grown accustomed to purchasing whatever we want when we want it. It is not easy to choose frugality over momentary pleasures. If you know you tend to buy on impulse, consider leaving your credit card at home. It is essential to identify destructive spending habits and look for ways to cut expenses - that expensive steak dinner that tasted so great this evening will likely be forgotten by tomorrow, that outfit we absolutely must have today might be out of date within a year and probably on its way to a local thrift store by the end of the year. Money dictates the flow of human living. Our belief about money is ingrained in us. A person who is stingy at fifteen is almost likely going to be tight at the age of fifty. If a frugal person has a relationship with a big spender, it is likely to cause him or her a great deal of stress. Similarly, it would if a super-tidy person lived with a chaotic and disorganised person. Couples should create a plan to generate income consistently, along with their financial goals and objectives. They can track their progress toward their goal monthly to see how well they are progressing with meeting their targets. By focusing on long-term goals, like buying a house, it can help take their mind of temporary discomfort.

## CREDITWORTHINESS

*"Whoever can be trusted with very little can also be trusted with much, and whoever is dishonest with very little will also be dishonest with much."* (Luke 16:10)

Every one of us has a credit file that gives a picture of our finances. Many people in a relationship are in more debt than they are willing to admit, a fact they often hide from their partner. Let me share a story with you. James and Rachel were planning their lives together, the wedding, as well as buying a house after the wedding. They found a beautiful three-bedroom home, which they could afford based on their income. However, their mortgage application was rejected because Rachel had a CCJ (County Court Judgement) on her credit file, which she didn't disclose to James. James felt a betrayal of trust and wondered what else she was hiding from him. If you are considering buying a property in joint names, this something you need to investigate before proceeding.

Marriage is a three-legged race. The person whom your leg is tied to would either slow you down, pull you up, or keep you on a steady pace in the race of life. There are signs your partner will show you of their creditworthiness; some are obvious, others are a bit more subtle. A man without a steady income, spending hundreds or thousands on a credit card, should tell you that he is a disaster waiting to happen. The question is, do you want to be a part of it? I dated a lady who told me to my face, "I will spend your money," confessing that she is a shopaholic. The irony of the situation was, at the time she made that comment, she lived in a shared house renting a room with her mother. She tried to cleverly pass her financial burden to me until I ended the relationship. We all fantasise about what it would be like to live like the rich and famous. Our Spending habits today tells a lot about what the future will be like. The fear of breaking up and starting over often keeps people in a bad relationship even though they can see the writing on the wall, "This is a disaster waiting to happen."

A lady seeking counsel from me asked, "Can I tell him everything about me?" In other words, should I go full disclosure or partial disclosure about my past and present? The answer to the question has many variables; as a rule of thumb, I asked what stage she was at in her relationship. I discussed the four stages of a relationship mentioned earlier in the book. Full disclosure is recommended when you are in the performing stage of your relationship. He or she has earned your trust and proven beyond any reasonable doubt that they are genuine and serious about a future together. The problem with a lie is that once you have told one, you have to tell another to cover the previous one, after a while, you might forget which version is the real truth.

Hope is not a strategy; living in denial is only postponing the inevitable. No human has the power to change the heart of another; only God reserves that right. However, we can learn new habits or skills that can make us a better money manager. There are symptoms of financial irresponsibility that we can identify early in the relationship if we know what to look for. A person who cannot manage a hundred pounds will struggle to manage a thousand. More money will only expose incompetence in handling money.

## MONEY MANAGEMENT STYLES

*"By wisdom, a house is built, and by understanding, it is established; by knowledge, the rooms are filled with all precious and pleasant riches."* (Proverbs 24:3-4)

There isn't a one-size-fits-all answer to every question. Knowing what each person brings to the table is essential, so no one feels exploited, unappreciated, or out of their depth. When couples become serious about their relationship, it is very important to discuss the money management style that suits them. There are many options available; I have highlighted five key styles.

**A Fully Joint Account:** The couple opens and operates a fully joint account. All income from both parties is paid into a single account. The fund required for living expenses (mortgage or rent, bills, loans) and projects (deposit for a house, holidays) will be drawn from this account at a specific date and time. This is advisable for young couples with similar incomes and just starting in life. It provides true accountability, the definition of naked, and not ashamed (see Genesis 2:25). If true transparency is the aim, then a fully joint account achieves that. The rule attached to the account must be followed; no one can withdraw from the account without prior notice or consent of the other party. It works particularly well when there is mutual trust between the couple or in a situation where the couple has different perceptions with regards to money; one party is more frugal, and the other person is a free-spender. This will curb the impulse to spend, or picking up bargains at the store, etc.

However, some people might view a fully joint account negatively, because it limits your personal freedom when it comes to your money. The rationale is that we used to have access to our money when we needed it; after all, we laboured for it. Secondly, if one party has a higher personal monthly commitment, such as a loan or credit card, then the other person might feel like they are carrying more than their fair share of the financial burden in the relationship. Thirdly, emergencies, or personal projects must be discussed and agreed before the fund can be released. You might opt to have an agreement for a personal allowance that can be spent without the need for consent; this will allow you to buy them a surprise gift without any eyebrows being raised. There aren't any hard and fast rules when it comes to a fully joint account. Couples simply have to agree on what works for them.

**Partially Joint Account:** Similarly, to using a fully joint account, the couple opens and operates an account for managing the expenses of the home. A certain percentage of their income is paid regularly into this account via standing order. The couple will have to agree on what bills must be paid from this account. This arrangement gives liberty to pursue personal projects from the rest of their income. Some people might still view this partial joint account negatively; if you are required to pay an equal percentage of your income, but you earn substantially more than your partner. You might feel it is unjust, especially if you are the lady. Secondly, what constitutes an emergency needs to be defined and evaluated on two criteria, personal or joint. If one party overspends their income the previous month, they might be unable to cover their bills in the new month. The joint account might be view as a slush fund to cover their excesses and habits.

**Split the Bill:** The third finance management style is to split the bills based on income and capacity. The couple makes full disclosure of their income to each other, and the bills are split accordingly. For example, the man could be responsible for mortgage or rent, insurance, etc. At the same time, the lady is responsible for the utility bills and council tax; this suggestion is for illustrative purposes only. In an unforeseen event such as one person losing their income, or they are unable to work due to sickness or illness, it might put a strain on the other person. In such cases, an adequate emergency fund or insurance should have been taken out, or put into place to cater for such eventualities.

**Save One and Spend One:** The fourth Finance management style is like a fully joint account, except it can be managed from two different accounts. The person with the lower income uses their income to pay all the bills, and the person with the higher income saves their income for a joint project, such as buying a house. All savings belong to both parties. The person who loves money and who is concerned only about personal profits does not hesitate to commit injustice. In an event where one party wants to break the agreement, the saving will be split equally or as agreed. Couples with this approach might opt for the savings to be paid into a fully joint account controlled by both parties.

**Do it all:** If your partner is very wealthy, he or she can volunteer to take care of all the bills. You are free of any commitment or obligation. You can live your dreams and do as you please with the money you earn. Although I do not advise this, I recommend that couples discuss each option carefully before proceeding to the next phase in their relationship.

## THE PRINCIPLE OF PARTNERSHIP – MINDSET AND MENTALITY

We all come from different backgrounds, and we all have different money mindsets. The question is, whose money is it? A man might say, "My money is mine, I worked for it, I earned it, and I can do with it whatever I want." A stay-at-home wife says, "No, it's our money. I take care of the house, cook the food, wash clothes, and if I weren't at home doing these things, you wouldn't have a home, so it's our money." A wife who also works says, "You have your money, and I have my money. What is yours is ours, and what is mine is mine". The question remains, whose money is it? Is it the husband's? Is it the wife's? The moment you say, "I do," the word "I" ceases to exist, it's now our money. Ego is a significant factor in decision making.

I have seen couples destroy their relationship over trivial things because they lack the common sense to sit down and discuss the way forward. There is no one-size-fits-all in marriage; every couple has to work their relationship in a manner that suits them and their pocket. The scriptures tell us, "The love of money is the root of all evil, but the lack of it, is a major cause of disagreement." (1 Timothy 6:10) Don't judge your life by what your friends are doing. It might surprise you that many of them are in debt to their eyeballs. They look good on the outside, but their bank statement tells a different story, many of us spend money we don't have merely to impress others. Life functions in seasons; we must all learn to crawl before we walk. We have a partnership in marriage! A husband and wife must be willing to work together financially, to share the responsibilities when these principles are employed, and work as a team to weather any financial difficulties. There is no room for selfishness in a marriage.

As Christians, our first financial partner is God. The Bible instructs us to give a tithe or give a tenth of our income to God (see Malachi 3:10). If you can trust God with your life, I don't see why you are struggling to trust Him with your money. You may be thinking, how can I possibly give a tenth, I am already struggling financially. I thought you were going to tell me how to get out of my financial challenges, but by doing this, I am only going deeper into debt. By giving God, the tenth you are securing the ninety with a blessing. After all, He owns it all (see Psalms 50:10). The truth is if we wait until all of our needs and wants are met before we start to tithe, we are not giving God a priority in our lives. I have not heard or seen anyone whose financial challenges got worse once they started to tithe; this is the secret of having more than enough. "It is God's blessing that makes us rich and adds no sorrow." (Proverbs 10:22) Put God first in your finances and see Him come through in every situation. It is one of the mysteries of God that works without fail.

Finally, I will encourage couples to invest in financial education. One of the advantages we have in the 21st Century is access to a wealth of information. There are thousands of online courses available to help couples educate themselves about finance and investing. Some schools and libraries offer free courses that you can take on from budgeting to investing. While you might not be planning a career as a financial investor, by becoming financially literate, you can understand investment basics. Thus, allowing you and your partner to make a smarter choice with your money and to increase your wealth. You can put every penny you scrimp to save into the right investment vehicle, which will continue to work for you year after year. The body of Christ is blessed with professionals such as solicitors, accountants, stock traders, etc. You can even pick up a thing or two just by having an informal conversation with them, then listen and learn as they share their knowledge. Lastly, invest in good books. I do recommend you read the classic book, "The Richest Man in Babylon," which will serve as an eye-opener on the subject of investing and money management.

Granted, life hits hard; despite our most diligent efforts, situations happen through no fault of our own. By focusing on where we want to be tomorrow, not simply what would make us happy today, we can make difficult financial decisions that keep us steadily toward our goals.

# REFLECTION QUESTIONS

1. Do you make enough to support a basic existence?
2. Have you decided on a chosen career path?
3. Where do you see yourself in five years in your career?
4. What kind of lifestyle do you want to live?
5. Have you grown in your chosen field, or do you feel stuck?
6. Are you concerned about financial security?
7. Do you have an emergency fund in place if you lose your job?
8. Did you consistently overspend monthly?
9. Is your partner faithful with his finances? Does he pay his bills on time?
10. Does your partner carry a lot of credit card debt?
11. Can your partner hold down a job?

# PRAYER POINTS

1. Father, thank you for not putting me in financial shame
2. Father, please forgive me for being a poor financial steward of the resources you have given me, or any poor decision and irresponsible purchases I have made in the name of Jesus
3. Father, give me the wisdom to manage my finances appropriately
4. Father, give me the wisdom to deal with any financial strife
5. Father, give me a teachable spirit on how to invest and manage money

# CHAPTER 5

# Tools for Conflict Resolution

A couple visited their Pastor for counselling on their marital challenge, hoping he will find a solution for them. The challenge was about the toilet seat being up or down. The lady wants the toilet seat down, while the husband leaves the toilet seat up. The couple often argued over the issue and did not speak to each other for days. The Pastor started by asking the lady, "Why do you want the toilet seat down?" The lady explained, "We have a two-year-old boy who is curious. If the toilet seat is up, he might put his hand into the toilet. For his safety, I want the toilet seat down." The Pastor asked the man the same question, "Why do you want the toilet seat up?" He replied, "I want convenience because I feel pain on my back from bending over." The Pastor replied, not taking anyone's side, but telling them they are both justified in their views. The couple looked at each other curiously. He offered a simple solution, "Get a lock on the door, where the child's hands cannot reach, this will stop the child from going into the toilet unsupervised, and it won't matter whether or not the toilet seat is up or down."—a simple solution, yet highly effective.

The sign of a great relationship is not a lack of conflict or disagreement. The reality is couples fight. They get on each other's nerves, hurt each other's feelings, and trigger each other in too many ways to count. Emotional depth is built by working through difficulties with your partner and not by running away when there is a conflict in the relationship. Our personality plays a crucial role in how we deal with conflict. If you're a temperamental or a sensitive person, a little criticism could trigger an adverse reaction; this will make you feel or think you are in the relationship with the wrong person. The thought to end the relationship and find someone who would agree with you all the time will be at the forefront of your mind. While this could be an easy option to take, you might be leaving "the devil you know for an angel you do not know." Storms in a relationship are inevitable; we would be living in denial if we thought we would never disagree with our partners. On a brighter side, conflict is an opportunity to express the way you feel and to reach a meaningful resolution with your partner. When we keep things that upset us inside, it does not help our relationship and makes us unhappy; it might act as a ticking time bomb.

This chapter aims to equip us with the tools to manage conflicts. If you are on the receiving end of a temperamental partner, you might think all hope is lost. You are willing to give in to their demands or comply with their request, your thought might sound like, "What do you want from me, just tell me, and I'll do it!" But in the process, you will accumulate resentment toward that person, or you lose your self-esteem. Every disagreement has one key ingredient, different points of view on the same issue; this varying viewpoint usually leads to conflict in relationships. We often hold onto some principles or values based on our personalities, cultures, heritage, education, affiliations, religious beliefs, etc. If we can identify the cause of the conflict, we will be equipped to move toward a resolution as opposed to merely going around in circles. When it comes to working through conflict with the people we care about; we must become better equipped to deal with the issue. A handyman who turns up at a job with only a hammer will make every problem a nail. We may be able to procrastinate over a lot of things in our lives, but you cannot afford to put off resolving a conflict. A conflict that is allowed to persist will ruin your relationship. It's like sitting on a keg of gun powder and playing with a match; you don't know when it might explode. Learning to see both points of view in a conflict is a great skill that many people lack; it's tough to see another person's point of view. There are certain subjects that we have already formulated our opinion on, we think we are right, and everyone else is wrong. The willingness to learn and acknowledge when we are wrong, or make mistakes, helps manage the ups and downs of any relationship. Then we can cut the number of conflicts we engage in with our partner.

# IMPROVED COMMUNICATION SKILL

*"A gentle answer turns away wrath, but a harsh word stirs up anger."* (Proverbs 15:1)

Communication is a critical skill that can be developed by every one of us. A part of effective communicating is knowing your intended audience and how your audience will understand it. Emerson Eggerichs, in his book, 'Love and Respect,' shared an essential insight into perception. He gave it a simplistic view that men see in blue, and women see in pink. In other words, the same message delivered the same way to different people will have different results. For example, if a man says, I have nothing to wear, it implies I have nothing clean to wear. If a lady says, I have nothing to wear; it means I have nothing new to wear.

It is crucial we know and understand how your partner receives information, the fulfilment of your vision rests on it. Perhaps a question we might consider asking ourselves is, "What am I trying to achieve by these words?" If it is their cooperation or motivation we are seeking, then our words and tone of voice must be carefully selected. There are four tones of voice that we use in a conversation, which are, Question, Statement, Command, and Sarcasm. Some people want you to be straightforward with them and not beat around the bush, while others like it in stages. Allow me to share an illustration titled; the dog is on the roof. One husband had not yet learned that his wife needed to be told things wisely. This husband and wife had a poodle that they loved very much. The dog was the object of their affection. One day, the wife began a trip that would take her to Europe on business. The first stop of her journey was in New York, where she got a connecting flight. When she arrived, she called her husband and asked how everything was at home. The man replied, "The dog is dead!" The wife was devastated. After collecting her thoughts, she asked her husband, "Why do you do that? Why can't you be more tactful?" He said, "Well, what do you mean by that? The dog died. How many other ways are there to say that?" The wife then said, "Well, you could give it to me in stages. For example, when I call from New York, you could say, 'The dog is on the roof,' and then when I travel to London the next day and call, you could tell me, 'Honey, the dog fell off the roof.' And when I call from Paris, you could add, 'Honey, the dog had to be taken to the vet. He's in the hospital, not doing well.' and finally, when I call you from Rome, 'Honey, brace yourself. Our dog died.' I could handle that." The husband responded, "Oh, I see." Then she asked, "By the way, how's mom?" After a moment's pause, the husband responded, "She's on the roof."

Trying to navigate the minefield of communication could be a difficult task. Most of us communicate reasonably well until we encounter disagreements, criticism, unreasonableness, or fundamental human differences. Learning to speak with wisdom and tact is an essential skill to have, not just in our romantic relationship but also in our professional lives. The bible records the story of Daniel, a captive under the rule of the ruthless and volatile Babylonian king named Nebuchadnezzar. He ordered that his wise men be killed because they could not tell him his dream and its interpretation. "When Arioch, the commander of the king's guard, had gone out to put to death the wise men of Babylon, Daniel spoke to him with wisdom and tact." (Daniel 2:14) Learning to improve our communication skills helps solve problems that confront us.

Allow me to share another illustration; a doctor hired a new secretary, who is very pretty with a model figure. A part of her responsibilities is to mail out the bills to all the doctor's patients. The doctor noticed that it was taking more time than necessary for her to fulfil this task, so he decided to observe her. He discovered that rather than using the wet sponge to seal the envelopes, she was licking each one. This activity elongated the time it took to mail the bill. The doctor asked her to use the sponge instead of licking each one, but the new secretary said that she would prefer to lick the envelope instead. The doctor tried all kinds of motivations to try and convince her to do things his way; he tried telling her how much quicker it would be, and that her mouth wouldn't get so dry. He even tried switching the type of envelopes that he used to the type that had sour-tasting glue. Nothing worked. One day, a patient came to the surgery to pay her bill and noticed that the secretary was licking the envelopes. She said to her, "Did you know that each envelope has about one and a half calories?" The secretary immediately stopped and began using a wet sponge. The patient knew how to get his point across with less effort.

If conflicts in relationships are inevitable, so is an apology. We all need to learn to speak our partner's apology language. There are times when words like "I am sorry" isn't enough. I want to share a story of a couple who came from different backgrounds and social status. The lady put a dent in her partner's car, and she had admitted responsibility for her actions. To show she was remorseful, she decided to write a poem to express how truly sorry she was. She noticed her partner did not respond; he proceeded with silent treatment toward her. She decided to ask him if she had done something else because she had tried to apologise and accepted responsibility for her action. She was shocked at his response. I did not receive an apology from you, and you did not accept responsibility. If you want to apologise and take the blame, you would have fixed my car. While some of us might condemn the request of the man toward his partner, we should take a step back and ask what he is trying to say. Gary Chapman and Jennifer Thomas wrote a book titled, 'Five languages of apology' in which they classify apology into five categories:

- **Expressing regret:** For many people, more than just saying I am sorry, we would like to see in the demeanour that the person who has injured us shows us regrets for their actions.
- **Accepting responsibility:** We can all find good reasons and explanations for why we behaved severely or did not come through on a commitment. Sometimes we might play the victim card or blame someone else for why things went the way they did. I think attitude is ingrained in our character, right from ancestor Adam (see Genesis 3:12-13). In addition to our words of apology is that we accept responsibilities for our actions.
- **Making Restitution:** The lady in the story returned her partner's car dented, and he felt a simple apology such as "I am sorry, it is my fault" did not suffice. It is crucial to bear in mind that they come from different social statuses. He might have other financial commitments, and adding the cost of fixing the dent might skew his budget for the month.
- **Genuinely Repenting:** An apology loses its sincerity if you give your loved one no assurance that you will try not to make the same mistake again. For some of us, and perhaps depending on the severity of the offence. A sincere apology requires that the person verbalise their desire never to hurt you in that way again. This is all you need to begin the healing and forgiveness.

- **Requesting Forgiveness:** Actions have consequences; within every human being is a desire for justice. To avoid retaliatory cycles, we need to admit our failure or to relinquish control and throw ourselves at the mercy of the injured party. It could be as simple as saying the words, "Will you forgive me?" This might be all it takes for healing and renewal of the relationship

Do you know your partner's apology language?

## BOUNDARIES

"And the Lord God commanded the man, "You are free to eat from any tree in the garden; but you must not eat from the tree of the knowledge of good and evil, for when you eat from it you will certainly die." (Genesis 2:16-17)

God first introduced the concept of boundaries in the scriptures when He placed man in the garden of Eden. While Adam kept within the confines of the limit, he was free to enjoy the benefits of the relationship. Then man fell from grace to grass when he overstepped the boundaries prescribed by God. In a romantic relationship setting up boundaries helps us to define who we are, what we want, and how we want to be treated by our partner. It also guides against the feeling of being used as a doormat.

Conflicts in a relationship often occur when boundaries are overstepped. An example, you communicated to your partner that you would not like him or her to go through your belongings without your consent. On one faithful day, you ordered takeaway food, while you were waiting for your order to be delivered, you fell asleep. The order arrived, and your partner decided not to wake you up but went through your wallet to pay for the food. Although he or she felt justified, when you woke up, you felt your boundaries had been overstepped. But your partner felt otherwise, what is the big deal? Why the secrecy? The reasoning behind your partner going against your boundary may not seem like a big deal to your partner, but it could be a big deal to you for whatever your reason might be.

Boundaries can make or break a relationship. You may feel that they are unnecessary because your partner is supposed to know what you want. With such assumptions come a lot of misunderstandings, because you are expecting your partner to read your mind or feel the same way you do. If you're unsure what your boundaries are, it's going to be hard for others to follow them. Your limits need to be well articulated. To help you define your boundaries, you must ask yourself, what is most important to me? What are my needs? How would l like to be treated? It could be as simple as you desiring honesty from your partner, no matter the situation that includes not deliberately omitting details of the event. They may also ask for the same in return. A poorly defined boundary in a relationship might alienate you from your partner and create a double standard. It will appear as if you are trying to manipulate the outcome of every conflict to your advantage by moving the goal post whenever it is convenient.

It is easy for us to perceive boundaries as a list of do's and don'ts or a means to control your partner. If you don't do X, I will hurt you by doing Y; this is the complete opposite of what boundaries are supposed to achieve. Boundaries aim to achieve mutual respect and taking into account one another's feelings. Boundaries are not a list of demands like I want the passwords to your phone or social media accounts, and if you don't give it to me, I will break up with you. If such demands are made in a relationship, this is a huge red flag. In a healthy relationship, you should not fear the consequences or feel obligated to give in to the demands of your partner. You should never feel afraid of your partner or their reactions irrespective of differences in opinion. If you make a sacrifice for someone you care about, it needs to be because you want to, not because you feel obligated or afraid of their reactions.

Setting and establishing healthy boundaries takes time, be respectful when sharing your thoughts and feelings with your partner so that you don't kill the spontaneity or dynamic of your relationship. Areas you might consider setting boundaries for include, intimacy, conflict engagement, and dealing with external relations. Partners should communicate with each other if their boundaries change. As a rule for engagement, when you disagree, it can be established that no name-calling, using derogatory terms, or bringing up past misdemeanours. If your boundaries are repeatedly crossed or disrespected, you must not ignore it. It is crucial to deal with it before you proceed to the next phase of the relationship. If you struggle to set boundaries while you still in a courtship, you will struggle to set boundaries when you get into marriage. Don't allow your affection to be won over with a gift at the detriment of your person; you might be like Esau selling his birthright for a meal.

# PICK YOUR BATTLES CAREFULLY

*"If someone slaps you on one cheek, turn to them the other also. If someone takes your coat, do not withhold your shirt from them."* (Luke 6:29)

At a time in my Christian journey, I misunderstood this bible verse because it contradicts my personality; no one likes to be a doormat or pushover. The principle behind the teaching is to encourage us to pick our battles carefully. Jesus demonstrated this principle in His life. During His arrest in the garden of Gethsemane, he is quoted saying, "Do you think I cannot call on my Father, and he will at once put at my disposal more than twelve legions of angels?" (Matthew 26:53) Those words demonstrate that He had power under control; in other words, humility. There are some battles in life; we have to lose if we want to win the war. A healthy relationship hinges on a couple's ability to know which issues are worth fighting over and which ones are worth letting go of. As a rule of thumb, "Don't fight a battle if you don't have anything to gain by winning." Conflict should be based on objectives rather than emotions. We demonstrate our maturity by knowing which battles to fight and which to walk away from. You might want to ask yourself these questions, what difference does winning make to my long-term goal? Will this issue matter to me in a month or a year? If you aim to marry your partner, how is calling her names or yelling going to achieve that? You need to take a step back and look at the bigger picture.

Our conscience, not our ego, should be our guide in choosing the battles we fight. We need a common denominator in any conflict; our ego versus logic. Ego and logic speak different languages, and no matter how loudly they shout at each other, they won't understand each other. I want to share a story of a newly wedded couple who got into a conflict, and within 12 months of their marriage, they were heading to a divorce court, their reason is 'an irreconcilable difference.' They sought counsel as a final attempt to salvage their marriage. The counsellor dug through a mirage of she did, I did, you said, he said and finally found the main issue. It all began with the toothpaste tube in the bathroom. He likes pushing the toothpaste from the bottom, and she likes pushing the toothpaste in the middle. The solution was to get a toothpaste tube with a release on top, which eliminates the need to push or pull from the middle or end.

Sometimes when we fight, we forget the objective of the battle. I am not asking you to run from every disagreement; if you believe in your heart, you need to disagree with your partner, then do so. There are things that you need to put in place during courtship that will be difficult to change when you are married. For example, one partner might be messier than the other. If you notice your partner throws his dirty socks on the floor around the house, you might want to discuss that as an issue before you say, "I do." Bear in mind disagreements don't have to be a shouting match. No one got into a relationship by being maltreated, and no one should accept being treated like a human punching bag. Our love account reached a romantic threshold before you felt the feeling of love for each other. Some people are in the habit of bringing a gun to a paper-knife fight. Learn to evaluate the downsides against the upsides of an issue with a clear mind before taking any drastic steps.

Life doesn't have to be a zero-sum game. The couple can have a win-win situation if this is what they desire. It is imperative to remember that you always have a choice in every conflict. You have the option to stop and walk away. Words are like eggs; once broken, it is impossible to put back together. Words exchanged during conflicts with your partner will be very difficult to take back once they have achieved the intended desire. Avoid hanging your dirty linen to dry in public; they will be used as tools against you in the future. Resist the urge to keep scores; keeping Scores assumes a winner and a loser. Always respond gracefully, particularly in the face of disgrace - it sees conflict as an opportunity to grow. Remember, in every battle, there is an opportunity to develop intimacy with your partner.

## COUPLES CONFLICTS TRIGGERS

*"If you know the enemy and know yourself, you need not fear the result of a hundred battles. If you know yourself but not the enemy, for every victory gained you will also suffer a defeat. If you know neither the enemy nor yourself, you will succumb in every battle."*
- Sun Tzu, Art of War

Most conflicts in a relationship can be avoided if we understand the triggers that set them off. A trigger can be something we do or say. Every one of us has something within us that triggers a negative emotion or reaction; it might be an old emotional wound, unresolved conflict, or a past traumatic event in our lives that we have buried, but not fully healed or overcome. It might sound like an obvious question; do you know what triggers negative emotion within you? What things get you worked up? Some triggers are real, and others merely a phase we are passing through in our lives. I encourage every couple to identify the triggers in their lives that cause negative emotions or reactions. Once we know each other's triggers, we agree not to pull or push them.

In this section, I want to highlight some common triggers for conflict in a relationship:

The first common trigger is Past Trauma and an Old Emotional Wound, which hasn't healed. I want to share a personal story with you. My flat was burgled many years ago, and after the event, I struggled with the feeling of retaliation and vengeance. I felt cheated by someone who had taken things of great value to me to buy drugs so that he can get high. To add salt to injury, the judge reduced the burglar's sentence on a technicality. I wanted blood. I carried the thought of retaliation and vengeance around for about a year, and any mention of burglary triggered pain and revenge within me. The pain was eating me from within. Before you ask, I was a Christian, I went to church, paid tithes, and served in the church as a musician. But one Sunday, I knelt at the altar, and I asked God to help me; that was the moment I let go of the pain and began to heal.

Some people in a relationship sometimes bring their past into the present. Perhaps they were poorly treated by their ex. When they see their new partner display similar behaviour to their ex, they become very defensive. For example, a simple request can become a trigger for a painful experience. A man asks his girlfriend, "Please, can you get me a glass of water?" She replies with a harsh tone, "Get yourself a glass of water. Am I your slave?" He is astonished by her refusal. She sees the request as an attempt to control her, just like an ex-boyfriend. She has vowed to herself she wasn't going to let that happen again. She has carried the past trauma into her new relationship. Until she heals from her past, she will not be able to develop a fruitful relationship with her new partner.

The Second common trigger is using Sensitive Information as a weapon. The relationship is about becoming vulnerable with your partner, being able to trust them with sensitive information about yourself, past failures, family history, and experiences. In a conflict, the couple needs to learn to fight fair, perhaps establish their rules of engagement. If one of the parties brings up any of this sensitive information as a means to hurt their partner, they end up opening an old wound, which will inevitably escalate the intensity and seriousness of the conflict. As a secondary effect, the party hurt won't trust his or her partner again.

The third common trigger is Harsh Criticism. No one likes being criticised harshly, especially when you feel you have given your best. If the criticism is public, it feels more like a humiliation. While I believe people should welcome constructive feedback, the couple needs to avoid belittling their partners. For example, a young lady might have some challenges with cooking specific food. As men, we might be used to experienced women cooking, such as mom or a local restaurant. Your partner might attempt to make you a meal, which turns out not as good as you would like it, be careful to keep your criticism of the meal to a minimum. Learn to appreciate the effort she put into it and give her time to perfect the skills needed.

On the other hand, some people don't like to be told when they're wrong, such attitude stifles the growth of the relationship, and it can create a very toxic environment. You will feel like you are walking on eggshells around your partner. I noticed very early in my relationship with my wife that her body language changes with my voice intonations. Her facial expression is like, "When you calm down, we can talk, at this point, I don't care." As soon as I learnt to adjust to how I give feedback to her, we were able to have a cordial relationship. If you are going to provide constructive feedback to your partner, take the time to select the choice of words carefully.

The fourth common trigger is Insensitive Response. Men are generally poor at reading women's emotions; they quickly dismiss or discard anything that doesn't match their macho perspective. For example, a lady might want to talk about her day with her partner, but all she gets is a one-word answer from him. This attitude isn't very reassuring to the lady because her partner would rather unwind playing video games or watching a sports game with his friends than spend time with her. She might feel that he is unconcerned with her emotional state, or he doesn't love her anymore. We discussed earlier in the book, the concept of love languages. Ladies generally like to spend quality time with their partner. Men, on the other hand, want to spend time alone watching a sports game or unwind with their friends. Their approach will create conflict in the relationship. A better approach to resolving this issue is to have a shared diary that allows the couple to have individual activities as well as joint activities.

The fifth common trigger is the feeling of being Unappreciated. Some people view dates like anniversaries or birthdays as essential, while others couldn't care less. Forgetting or missing an important date, such as a birthday, might trigger the feeling of being unappreciated by your partner. I would confess and say I am not a birthday person, but I have managed to remind myself by using a calendar system to remind myself of important dates. You might hear your partner say, "It is the thought that count, the gift doesn't matter." I will give you a clue; in most cases, the gift does matter. If you find yourself forgetful of essential dates, set up a simple reminder system on your smartphone. It helps you stay one step ahead. On many occasions, our partner asks us to do something, which requires us to go out of our way. Remember to say, "thank you" in such situations to show that you appreciate the effort they have put into getting a gift or making your life a little more comfortable.

The sixth common conflict trigger is the feeling of being Taken Advantage of. Some people take kindness as a weakness, and therefore they see an opportunity to exploit. I took a lady who was travelling to the airport. She carried four extra baggage, in addition to the two baggage she was allowed on the flight. She knew the additional baggage incurred costs. At the airport, she expected me to pay for the four extra baggage she carried without any prior notice to me. While responsibilities in a relationship are rarely shared equally, it is important that partners don't take each other for granted and make an effort to contribute when they can. No one likes a freeloader. It creates a feeling of resentment and lack of trust in the relationship.

The seventh common conflict triggers are Wandering Eyes. The scriptures say, "I made a covenant with my eyes not to look lustfully at a young woman." (Job 31:1)
This is more applicable to men than women. Men are visual and innately drawn to a pretty woman. They may take a glance at someone attractive; this is probably an involuntary action, but it shows a lack of discipline. Being in a committed relationship doesn't make a person suddenly impervious to attractive people. The relationship is

a commitment, and love is a decision we have to make daily. If your partner catches you in the act, it might lead to a conflict. It might make your partner feel unattractive to you; this can bring up feeling insecurity and even suspicion, "Does he find her more attractive than me?" While I hope you are not expecting your partner to wear blinders like a racehorse, it is not unreasonable to request that he or she respect you when they are around other people.

Secondly, I encourage you to feel confident in your beauty. Your partner must have found something attractive in you before you got into a relationship. We are beautifully and wonderfully made (see Psalm 139:14). You should be able to recognise beauty in others. In other words, she's beautiful, and so am I. It shows that you are confident in yourself and your relationship; this might be a better way to deal with the issue than drawing attention to it. It is human nature to notice when an attractive person walks by, so when it happens, don't read too much into it.

The eighth common conflict trigger is an Ex coming back into your life. There are times when your ex may come back into your life for whatever reason. It could be a friendly text message, email, or phone call. Your partner might see this as a threat and become territorial. If you have unfinished emotional business with this person, it could be bait, especially if the relationship did not end on bad terms. When an ex makes an entrance in your life, you must decide very quickly what type of relationship you want from them. If jealousy is aroused in your partner, it will fracture the trust in the relationship. Your partner might start connecting imaginary dots or beliefs about your fidelity. Once these fanciful thoughts are planted, they become impossible to shake off. Avoid taking private calls from your ex; it will only lead to suspicion.

The ninth common conflict trigger is Unresolved Conflict. Couples must learn to discuss their feelings before it becomes too emotionally charged. When we bottle up our feelings and thoughts within us, it carries the enormous risks of blowing up unexpectedly. Since no one wants to discuss the issue, we try to ignore it or sweep it under the carpet. However, the result is a rollercoaster of the same fight on a different night, until someone decides to be the matured one and discuss the elephant in the room. You need a clear objective before engaging in a conversation, or nothing will get resolved. It is essential to see your partner's perspective on the issue, rather than your own, if you want a lasting solution.

The tenth common conflict trigger is the feeling of being Disrespected. This trigger often occurs when boundaries are crossed repeatedly. For example, when you feel your personal space is being invaded by your partner but an attempt to discuss it as an issue is quickly shut down. Sometimes your partner cuts you off mid-sentence with regards to the issues at hand as if your opinion is not valued in the relationship. It is necessary to remember that respect is synonymous with admiration. If one of the couples continues to repeat this negative pattern, he or she will ultimately damage the relationship beyond repair.

## ARE YOU A PEACEMAKER OR A PEACEKEEPER?

*"Blessed are the peacemakers for they will be called children of God."* (Matthew 5:9)

The difference between a peacemaker and peacekeeper is shown when there is a disagreement, the peacekeeper often retreats. They allow a lot of small issues to pile up until it becomes a problem. Due to their personality type, they don't want to rock the boat or risk tension in a relationship. They want the relationship to work at all costs, even if they are unhappy. They often turn the other cheek when they are upset. Peacekeepers are concerned about the present peace than the long-term survival of the relationship. While a peacemaker aims for reconciliation, he or she understand that dealing with issues as they arise keeps them small, keeps the slate clean, and builds an environment of trust where no one is waiting to be blindsided by someone blowing up at them. If a Peacekeeper blows up, their partner might wonder, "Where did that come from?" They have often gotten away with much more.

Peacekeepers often misunderstand the definition of peace, which doesn't mean the absence of conflict. If you avoid conflict in the name of peace, the peace you keep will be superficial and fragile. We must learn to keep harmony in the relationship with our partner even when we disagree with them. My wife and I agreed that we wouldn't discuss any hot conversation; we will wait for it to cool down. This doesn't stop us from getting on with other things while we wait. It might take a few hours or a day. I found this to work effectively, especially when we see the issue from two perspectives. Experience has taught me that in the heat of the moment, you end up saying things you might be unable to take back.

In our professional lives, we have learnt to disagree with our colleagues and still go out to lunch with them without any issue or verbal altercation. These conversations are kept as two parallel lines that don't meet. This skill is transferable into our relationship; we must learn to deal with our pain and anger without ruining the relationship with our partners. However, this is a challenge for people having a people pleaser personality; they frequently suppressed their opinion in an attempt to avoid conflict. We're going to find ourselves in battle. What matters is how we deal with conflict in our relationships when the friction comes. In other words, learn to weather the storm together and also enjoy the sunshine. The Scriptures tell us, "Bear with each other and forgive whatever grievances you may have against one another. Forgive as the Lord forgave you." (Colossians 3:13)

To be successful, there are some steps you can take to secure peace with others.

1. Attack the problem, not the person. Laying out an annotated history of your spouse's shortcomings is counterproductive and simply fuels the fire. When fighting, don't wander into other unaddressed issues before the current one is resolved.
2. Cooperate whenever possible. Look for common ground. Have rules of engagement. Rules are helpful on so many levels. You must recognize fighting as a natural part of the relationship. It formalizes the premise that you're not interested in playing the blame game and outline safe parameters for working out issues. One man said to his wife, "How could you be so beautiful and so stupid at the same time?" She said, "That's easy. God made me beautiful, so that you would be attracted to me. He made me stupid, so I'd be attracted to you."
3. Emphasize reconciliation, not resolution. Avoid resentment and build-up by dealing with your pain and anger as soon as possible. When you rehearse and replay what happened over and over, you continue to hurt yourself.

In every chaos, there is an opportunity. Conflict can be a healthy stepping stone to an improved relationship. To be an effective peacemaker, you must understand the apology language of yourself and your partner.

In almost every relationship, there is a person who plays the role of a peacekeeper.
The peacekeeper typically is the first person to break the silence when there is a disagreement or to apologise, even if they are not at fault. The challenge with such an approach in a relationship is that resentment often builds in their heart, and in an unexpected moment, there is an outburst of anger.

## REFLECTION QUESTIONS

1. "Why am I so reactive to that particular behaviour of my partner? Why does that one thing bother me so much?"
2. What triggers negative emotions within me?
3. How did I manage emotion before?
4. Do you ever feel like people take advantage of you or use your emotions for their own gain?
5. Do you spend a lot of time defending yourself for things you believe aren't your fault?

# **PRAYER POINTS**

1. Father, thank you for the presence of the Holy Spirit in my life and granting me the grace to rule over my spirit
2. Father, help me mature the fruit of the Spirit in my life
3. Holy Spirit, help me to deal with emotional issues that are unresolved in my past
4. Father, help me to see the boundaries in my relationship
5. Father, equip me with the tools to deal with the challenges of my relationship

# CHAPTER 6

# Dealing with your Partners' Relations

*"Likewise, every good tree bears good fruit, but a bad tree bears bad fruit. A good tree cannot bear bad fruit, and a bad tree cannot bear good fruit."* (Matthew 7:17-18)

Like father, Like Son, Like Mother, Like Daughter, we inherit a lot of features from our parents. Genes and facial features are made up of our parents but, more importantly, our attitude to life, values, and personality.

Spending time with your potential future in-laws will allow you to uncover the things your partner might try to hide in their nature and character while you are in a relationship. For example, if the lady's mother is very bossy and likes to dominate her husband. Guess what; there is a very high probability that your future wife will be very bossy and want to dominate you.

Suppose the man's father is unethical with a shallow spiritual foundation. Guess what; there is a very high chance that the man you are with will lack ethics and be shallow spiritually.

Apples don't fall far from the tree; a child usually behaves in a similar way to his or her parents. Some years ago, I was driving back from church with a deaconess at the church I attended; she made a profound statement that evening, she said, "If you ever wish to marry a lady, always look at the mother before you do." Those words unlocked a pearl of wisdom in me; your partner's parent is the present example of what your future spouse will be like. When a young man or woman tries to avoid meeting or seeing their partner's parents, they are merely robbing themselves of the opportunity to see what the future will be like for them.

Yes, there are exceptions to the rule of Like Father, Like Son, Like Mother, Like Daughter. In some cases, sons don't act like their fathers or daughters like their mothers. But this is a rare occurrence; the norm is that a child typically follows the patterns of their parents.

## FAMILY STRUCTURE

Our definition of family adds additional complexity to the relationship. Someone might consider Uncles, Aunts, and cousins a part of the family, while others prefer to keep it simple. Sometimes couples feel torn between two worlds, i.e., defying their family or their partner. Parents often want their children to uphold their traditions, religious beliefs, politics, social class, caste system, which is very important to them. I do firmly believe in parental blessings before two people in love say "I do" to each other. If you're strongly attached to your family, there is a risk that your joy will be dependent on the joy of your family. It can become suffocating to the growth of the relationship or the new life you are trying to build with your partner.

Managing the relationship with in-laws is easier said than done. Meeting your future in-laws for the first time might feel like a daunting task. We want it to be perfect since we don't get a second chance at making a first impression. Like a job interview, you must take your time to prepare for a meeting; learn about their norms and family values before the visit. You have a good source of information in your partner, who is already a member of the family. If your partner is reluctant to share information about his or her family, it might be an indication of underlying issues, try to probe but don't push, as this might make him shut down completely. Be prepared to answer questions about yourself and your family. It is also an opportunity for you to ask questions and deepen your knowledge of the kind of family you are about to join.

While we are all raised in different family structures, for example, some people are raised by two parents, while others are raised with a single parent, step-parent, relatives (grandparents, uncles, etc.), or even foster parents. The family structure in which we are raised plays a significant role in our development and how we view relationships and marriage. Structures are necessary for marriage because they keep the building upright in a storm. When a young adult has no father or mother figure in their lives, it can be like a ship at sea without any sight of the lighthouse. You must decide from the onset before you exchange vows what kind of structure you want in your marriage.

The structure in place determines how you manage the home. What I mean by structures are simply agreements or compromises reached with your partner before you were married. In some cultures family members turning up on your doorstep unannounced is acceptable, and you might consider it as an intrusion, but this might be what it means to be part and parcel of the family. You might prefer that they call first before showing up on your doorstep. There are other topics worth considering, such as a member of the family staying with you after marriage. It is one thing if they visit once a year for a holiday; it's another if they are living with you, and there is no set date as to when they will be leaving.  It would be best if you discussed this with your partner; there isn't a one-size-fits-all answer. Economic backgrounds play an important role, too. If your partner is the breadwinner in his family, the chance is he or she will be responsible for the wellbeing of his or her family even after you are married.

We all make mistakes; there are things in our past we are not proud of. A young lady felt betrayed by her husband of seven years when she discovered he had a son before marrying her. The discovery was made known to her by a third party, which add more salt to the injury. She confronted him and found that it was true. She contemplated her next step, including divorce. But they both sought for counsel, and she decided against divorce, but she felt she could not trust him anymore. Courtship is a discovery phase of the relationship. A child outside of marriage should not be a deal-breaker. However, an open and honest discussion is needed in the relationship. You must consider if you are ready for the responsibility of being a step-parent before you have your children.

## HELP MY FUTURE MOTHER IN LAW IS A WITCH

*"Honour your father and mother," this is the first commandment with a promise."* (Ephesian 6:2)

Don't be swayed by stereotypes and stigma that comes with mothers-in-law; it states, "All mothers-in-law are witches." Your friends and family can introduce subtle poison into your heart, which clouds your judgement and thinking when it comes to your relationship with your mother-in-law. Make an effort to observe and understand your future in-laws, then respond or judge the situation accordingly.

Ladies, if you get the feeling your future mother-in-law doesn't like you, it may come from outright disapproval during your visit or subtle criticism. There are ways to build a relationship with your future mother-in-law. But trying to separate a mother and son is not only unwise but also diabolical for two essential reasons, you are asking for a formidable enemy. I mentioned earlier in the book that you must learn to pick your battles carefully. Please, don't put your partner in a situation where he has to choose between you and a relative. If the physical umbilical cord is severed, the spiritual and emotional cord is not. Mothers are the go-to person for their sons; they had established a relationship long before you came on the scene.

Even if you win the battle, you will ultimately lose the war. It would be best if you had her as an ally, not as an enemy. Secondly, you reap what you sow (see Galatians 6:7). If you plan to be a parent in the future, the seed you sow today will germinate and bring a harvest. If you wish your future mother-in-law dead today, your son's partner will also wish you dead or try to put a wedge between you and your son. The partner is not seen as the 'first' woman in the man's life until you are married. It appears as if you are competing for the affection of the same man. Hence, you have to be very patient. Most mothers-in-law seek a relationship like that of Ruth and Naomi (see Ruth 1: 16-18). Remember, a relationship is a two-way street, and you might be amazed at how different your relationship can be if you focus on her feelings and thoughts instead of your own.

The first step in forging a relationship with your future mother-in-law is to understand her perspective. When a mother looks at her son, what she sees is her baby boy. She brought him home from the hospital many years ago, she cared for him, carried and nursed him at her side. She has also spent her whole life (time, energy, and resources) nurturing and protecting him from strangers and dangers. Her first impression of you is that you're a stranger trying to steal her son away, and she has to defend him. Don't fuel her suspicion by your inexperience of attempting to drive a wedge between a mother and her son. You have simply declared war. He is your man, and I would agree, but before he became a man, he was a baby, who became a little boy and then a man. The process required someone caring for him. Think of it as an investment made by his mother, which she wants to guard jealously. The correct approach would be spending some time with her to build up trust and encourage her to return the favour. When you are planning to marry, you are not marrying the man or woman alone, but their entire family.

Tensions with mothers-in-law are typical, but with time fear can be replaced with friendship and mutual respect. I do caveat this statement by saying, there are some outliners in a relationship where the mother-in-law can be very controlling and shows no respect to you no matter how much you try. Generation X, Y, and Z refer to people born in different eras; this dramatically affects the perspective on what we consider as the norm. In our day's email is one of the fastest means of communication, in the previous generation, the mail post was the fastest. My point is, you might not see eye to eye because you are looking at things from two different perspectives.

Finally, learn to hold your tongue, sometimes telling the whole truth can do more damage than good. Don't talk negatively about yourself or your family in front of the future in-laws, be gracious with your words even if there is tension at home. Don't make your first visit, your last visit except in exceptional circumstances. Evaluate your visit to future parent-in-law; it helps you plan for the kind of boundaries you want to establish in your marriage.

## INTERRACIAL MARRIAGE

*"There is neither Jew nor Gentile, neither slave nor free, nor is there male and female, for you are all one in Christ Jesus."* (Galatians 3:28)

Interracial relationships are a difficult topic to discuss, even for Christians. Some ultra-conservative Christians have found bible verses to justify why two people from a different race or ethnic group cannot marry; this is based on personal agenda or prejudice. God warns His people not to intermarry with certain people. He forbade the children of Israel to intermarry with the Canaanites (see Deuteronomy 7:3), but this was for spiritual reasons, not racial reasons. You might recall that Solomon, the wisest king, went from loving the Lord to loving strange women when he intermarried with other nations (see 1 Kings 3:3, 1 Kings 11:1). God frowned at racial discrimination; He dealt severely with Aaron and Miriam's racial prejudice against Moses's wife (see Numbers 12:1-10). He did not condone it. People seeking justification using the scriptures for racial discrimination are merely twisting the facts for personal reasons. God doesn't look at our skin colour; He is more interested in our hearts. God is no respecter of person, colour, or ethnicity. However, a couple in an interracial relationship must be prepared to make a lot of self-sacrifices and put in hard work to surmount external barriers or influences, which could drive them apart. It is essential that couples remain focused on their primary reason for being together.

One of the challenges that come with interracial relationships is identity. Who do you identify yourself with? Who will your children identify themselves with? Most people derive their identity from their race. If one of the couples is very traditional and also very stubborn, there will be clashes over the loss of identity, which can undermine the strength of the relationship. I offer the solution that your identity is now in Christ, not in the colour of your skin (see 2 Corinthians 5:17). The power of the Gospel breaks down the barrier of race because we have all been adopted into the same family of God. Each believer has more in common with another believer than race, culture, and tradition.

God loves diversity and uniqueness. Our race plays a significant role in our relationship, more than we choose to admit. How we express love is more than just the chemistry we have with our partner; it is how we have been shaped by our race, ethnicity, or culture. Traditionally in the west, when you take a lady out on a date, you are expected to open the door of the car for her or buy her flowers. In some cultures, around the world, if a man does such a thing, he would be considered weak. The world has become a global village; there is a higher chance that we would fall in love with someone other than our kin. I am not asking you to be colour blind, but be well equipped with the tools to deal with the challenges ahead.

## CULTURE

The movie "My Big Fat Greek Wedding" highlights the differences in cultures in our society. Culture plays an integral part in our lives, and if you choose to marry, your partner's culture becomes a part of your life. It's easier for you to defend your culture and make assumptions about your partner's culture. Most people grew up with stereotypes about other people's cultures; our upbringing has conditioned us to think in a particular way. If your partner has a different culture to yours, you must take the time to learn what the differences, misconceptions, and even biases about their culture are. The more you get to know about your partner's culture, the easier it becomes to understand your partner.

In cross-cultural relationships, habits, rituals, and beliefs are so diverse that it's impossible for you or your partner to adopt every single aspect of each other's culture. You need to learn to compromise, adjust to each other, and have mutual respect. The best thing is that you both have the opportunity to pick the best of both worlds that make both of you happy, and no one culture is superior to another. Like any couple, your relationship is built on the similarities you have as individuals, not the differences cultures may have. Humans are not magnets, so opposites do not attract.

The myth that "love conquers all" is precisely that; it is just a Myth. What we perceive as male and female roles are greatly affected by our cultures. In some cultures, the woman is expected to cook and wash the dishes; in other cultures, the lady expects that if she cooks, then the man should wash the dishes. Many disagreements stem from a lack of understanding of the cultural background. A simple conversation about house chores or who is doing what before you get married will eliminate a lot of wrong assumptions.

The food we eat is also engrained in our culture. While you are dating, eating in a restaurant, and getting a takeaway might be the norm. However, this will drastically change once you are married. Trying something new could be fun, but might not be practical for everyday routine. Some people like hot and spicy food, while others eat mild-tasting food, some eat meat while others do not. Perhaps, make the time to visit your partner's home country. It could be expensive and time-consuming, but this is a sacrifice for love, and it helps you to understand the culture a bit better.

The language we speak also adds a layer of complexity; most people feel more comfortable speaking in their mother tongue when they are around members of their family or friends. If you don't understand your partner's mother tongue, you might feel isolated. If they crack a joke among themselves, you might feel they are talking about you; this can be an awkward moment. Take the chance to learn from your partner his or her mother tongue, at least understand some words, so you don't feel completely alienated.

Finally, are you moving to your partner's country? The thought of living abroad sounds fun. But what do you do when you feel homesick? A lady fell in love with a man from the Middle East during their post-graduate studies, they planned to get married, and he was expecting her to move back to his country with him. She jumped on the idea of living abroad without thinking through the details. Within two weeks of moving into a new country, she quickly realised it wasn't a holiday but an entirely new life. It was a major culture shock; she was expected to dress, pray, and worship in a particular way. She became homesick and wanted to return home. But her new husband was not willing to move back; he had a great job and life in his own country. In this type of situation, there is no easy way out. Topics such as where are we going to live once we are married, must be discussed in great detail before the, "I do."

## REFLECTION QUESTIONS

1. What type of relationship do you have with your parents?
2. Who is your father or mother figure?
3. What kind of structure do you want in your marriage?
4. How do we manage extended family relationships?
5. Do you have any children?
6. What kind of boundaries do you want in place for family members?
7. What are your personal beliefs on interracial marriages?
8. What are your family beliefs on interracial marriages?

# PRAYER POINTS

1. Father, thank you for the wisdom to deal with difficulty and challenging relationships in my life
2. Father, the mistake of my parent, will not be repeated in my life in Jesus' name
3. Father, grant me the wisdom to live peacefully with my new family
4. Father, grant me the grace to communicate with my partner effectively
5. Father, help me identify the pitfalls that destroy relationships with my family

# CHAPTER 7

# Don't Marry a Stranger

How well do you know your partner? The depth of your knowledge and breadth of your experiences with your partner before marriage plays a significant role in the success of the marriage. One of the worst feelings you can have is to wake up one morning in bed with your spouse, look at him or her and say to yourself, "I don't know this person." My spouse isn't the flawless person I married. Within a few weeks or months after the honeymoon, you will start to notice the imperfections in your spouse. The feeling of anger fills your heart; the key is how you respond and resolve your disappointment; it is challenging to keep the marriage growing if we focus on the negative. We tend to do our due diligence in other aspects of our lives, like buying a new car or a house. We would check the history of the vehicle, how often it was serviced, has it been in an accident, the mileage, performance on the motorway and in the city, is there any warranty, etc. These questions and many more give us a better idea of the vehicle we are about to buy and saves us from potential future headaches. The more information we have, the better decision we can make. Don't feel pressured to marry someone you do not know; the truth is, you will have to carry the consequences alone. A proposal doesn't have to be 'yes,' it can be a 'maybe' let us get to know each more, or a 'no.' You always have a choice.

I would like to share a story of Josh and Mary with you. Josh is a 37-year-old eligible bachelor who resides in New York. He is a tall, dark, and handsome, and a successful businessman. You can define him as an ideal bachelor. He went on holiday to his home country to visit his parent and to begin a few projects. On his arrival, he met a lady at his parent's residence who introduced herself as Mary. He exchanged pleasantries with her, but Josh's mother mistook Josh's benevolent attitude to Mary as a sign of interest in her. She made it her duty to sing her praises to him at every opportunity and highlighted her good qualities. She mounted the pressure on him to get married as she was desperate for grandchildren. She wasn't willing to give her blessings if he married a lady who was not from his home country. Josh shrugged off his mother's suggestions, but his mom wouldn't let the matter rest.

Mary is a 32-year-old well-educated lady, but she has never been outside her home country. Her knowledge of the United States is from stories, movies, and books. She particularly hates the cold winter often describe by people visiting from the United States, so she has no interest in living outside her home country. However, Josh's mother hinted to Mary's mother about Josh's interest in Mary. The two mothers were ecstatic to see their children married. Josh was only visiting for two weeks. The two mothers added pressure on their children to be in a relationship, encouraging the new forced couple to get married as soon as possible, citing their age and fertility as significant factors. Josh and Mary proceeded quickly through the rank of dating and courtship, most of which was done via phone calls, and Josh's occasional visit to the country. They got married, and Mary was reluctant to move abroad, citing she had a life in her home country, and she was happy. Josh doesn't want to leave the United States, he has a business to run, and he was successful. They were at a standstill; the pressure of both parents could not make either party budge from their stance. The compromise was that they visit each other as often as possible throughout the year.

## DIFFICULT CONVERSATIONS

*"Therefore confess your sins to each other and pray for each other so that you may be healed."* (James 5:16a)

I would like to share a story of a couple who have been married for a few years and unable to conceive and have a child. They had multiple medical examinations, and the doctor confirmed that they were both fine medically. They were Christians, so they prayed and fasted, believing in God to do a miracle. They became anxious in their wait, and so they decided to see their Pastor and booked an appointment for a Counselling session. They arrived on the date of their meeting, the Pastor prayed with them, and he spoke by the Spirit of God and asked the couple, "If they have ever had an abortion?" It was quite strange to ask such a question of a couple who is wanting a child. But the atmosphere in the room changed, and the woman began to cry; the man was remorseful with his head bowed. You would think it is strange for a couple desiring the fruit of the womb to have had an abortion. The story goes like this, while the couple was in courtship, the woman got pregnant, they knew the church would not wed them if they were pregnant. They decided to terminate the baby with the hope that they will have more children once they are married. Unknown to the man, when he goes to work, the woman stays at home crying herself to a stupor, she does this, day in and day out, feeling guilty of her part in the abortion. The effect of the mind on the body has affected their ability to conceive (psychosomatic). The Pastor encouraged them and prayed with them, assuring them that the blood of Jesus washes away all sin (see 1 John 1:8-10). Within three months, the couple was expecting their first child.

The story above can be viewed in multiple scenarios. It could be the man with skeletons in his cupboard he has not dealt with, or it could be the lady with asecret from her past she cannot reveal— some realities we need to face sooner rather than later. Deal with your pain, sorrow, and secrets before they become larger than life. God's principle is that we reap what we sow is always in effect (see Galatians 6:7).

One of the hardest things for anyone to do is to admit that they are struggling in a particular area of their life. Many young Christians suffer from addictions, substance abuse, pornography, etc. They try to cover it up, play it down or ignore it, but it doesn't go away. The challenge we have in our lives, which is not dealt with today, will come out and trip us up in the future. Many marriages have been broken because couples have failed to identify their weaknesses before they say, "I do." One of the hardest sentences is to say, "I have a challenge in this area of my life, and I need help." It takes a lot of maturity and courage to admit that you are struggling in a particular area of your life. You might be able to get away with blaming someone else; eventually, when there is no one else to blame, you will realise that you are the constant factor in the equation. We have a few examples in the scriptures:

Moses had an anger problem, but yet the Bible calls him the meekest man on earth (see Numbers 12:3). Righteousness in one area does not justify sin in another. You might be a worship leader in your church, an usher, or the pastor; it doesn't excuse your weaknesses. There were glimpses of anger issues early in the life of Moses, which eventually cost him the Promised Land (see Numbers 20:12). He killed a man he felt maltreated his fellow countryman (see Exodus 2:12), he smashed the Ten Commandments when he saw the people worshipping the idol (see Exodus 32:19), he struck the rock with his rod when he was commanded to speak (see Numbers 20:11). We can whitewash everything Moses did, even provide valid reasons; it was the people he led that murmured, complained, and irritated him for 40 years. He simply got to his breaking point and let loose. In the end, Moses alone bore the consequences of his action, not the people. Anger demands a reaction. It wants you to throw caution to the wind, say what you want to say and do what you feel like doing. There are ways to control your emotions; if you have a weakness, learn to control it before it destroys a lifetime of work, including your marriage.

Samson is another example; he was like a rock star in his day. However, he struggled to control himself with women. He is the only man in the Hall of Faith in Hebrews 11, who slept with a prostitute (see Judges 16:1); this is not a great testimony. You might wonder where he got the taste for this even though he was filled with the Holy Spirit. Similarly, many Christians today have a taste for the things of the world. We want to act and talk like they do. Samson did not deal with the challenge of fornication, and the same problems he refused to deal with brought him down. He committed suicide, killing his enemies (see Judges 16:30). We must humble ourselves and not be deluded by thinking we have attained mastery of things, that we have simply covered up.

## UNDERLYING HEALTH ISSUES AND CONDITIONS

The little foxes spoil the Vine.

Matt and Olivia were just a few weeks away from their wedding day, the wedding plans were in full steam, and everyone was very excited. They were advised by their Pastor to take a genotype test as a precautionary measure. The couple was shocked to find out they were both AS genotype. It was a deal-breaker, and the wedding plans had to be halted. One of the health issues that need to be discussed by the couple intending on marrying is the genotype. Genotype can refer to a gene or set of genes carried by an individual. Every one of us belongs to one of four genotypes, which are AA, AS, AC, SS, and from the four groups, we can have a variation of combinations. Most adults don't know their genotype or haven't been bothered to check. While I am a man of faith, I believe it is better to know and understand the challenges you are facing than praying aimlessly.

Often couples overlook health topics because most young adults are relatively healthy and in love. Our generation has seen an increase in cases of cancer, diabetes, HIV, STDs, etc. Many factors are responsible for this, from our daily diet to our lifestyle. One of the saddest things I have witnessed is a parent burying their children in the prime of their lives. Medical technology, today, is so advance that we can get the results of our test in a matter of minutes, so there is no excuse not to get tested for common diseases or illnesses. The danger of an AS genotype carrier marrying another AS genotype carrier is that there is a high probability of one or all of their children carrying a SS genotype (Sickle Cell). The quality of life for the SS genotype carrier is sometimes very poor. The most compatible genotype is an AA marrying an AA, you save your future children the worry about genotype compatibility. I recommend that you seek medical advice; I am not a trained medical practitioner.

## DO YOU PLAN TO HAVE CHILDREN?

A couple sat in the counselling room with their Pastor; they were beaming with joy as their wedding was a few days away. The Pastor asked the couple a question in a humorous way, "How many children do you plan to have?" The couple spoke simultaneously. She said, "None," and he said, "Five." There was an awkward silence in the room. The lady doesn't want anything to hinder her career aspirations as she plans to climb the corporate success ladder as quickly as possible. Moreover, she comes from a home where she is the only child. But the man wants a big family, and not having children of his own seems sacrilegious. Couples often ignore the conversation about having children until it is too late because they have made the wrong assumption about their partner's desire for children. While the cost of having, raising, and educating a child could be astronomical, it is crucial that the couple discuss the subject of having children as soon as they know that their destination is 'happily ever after.' Living out your marital dreams in the real world can be difficult. In this example, we had two spectrums of people who operate in the extreme, which range from "I do not want children at all," to "I want as many as possible." Others want to wait a few years before having children.

A common complaint is the difficulty of finding someone to care for the children while both parents are at work. A Potential solution is to leverage the use of technology capabilities of the Internet and flexible working hours that are common in today's world. Parents can have offices at home and schedule their work hours as per the needs of their children. It can save a considerable amount of money for childcare, which happens to be one of the biggest expenses incurred on an ongoing basis.

The issue of the sex of the baby is sometimes a bone of contention. Perhaps, though, not as common in the 21st century. I have seen cases where the family of the man, put pressure on their son to marry a second wife so that he can have a male child. The issue of the wife unable to produce a male child stems from a lack of understanding of genetics. The biologist explains to us that the man is responsible for the sex of the baby. A woman produces XX chromosomes, while the man produces XY chromosomes. For a male child, you need XY and a female child you need XX; the woman will supply the X chromosome, and the male produces the Y chromosome. The pressure placed on the woman is not only unfair but unreasonable; she cannot influence the sex of the baby. Couples are encouraged to discuss their preference with regard to the sex of the baby.

# DO NOT BE YOKED TOGETHER WITH UNBELIEVERS

*"Do not be unequally yoked together with unbelievers. For what fellowship has righteousness with lawlessness? And what communion has light with darkness?"* (2 Corinthians 6:14)

The truth is that we cannot avoid unbelievers altogether, we have to engage with unbelievers at work, the gym, the park, and social events, etc. What Paul is referring to here is a principle established in the Old Testament, where God forbade ploughing your field with an ox tied to a donkey. The reason is that the ox not only does all the work but also has to drag the donkey around all day. This makes the work of the ox much harder than it needs to be; the relationship is unequal (see Deuteronomy 22:10). When a believer is in a relationship with an unbeliever, it will prevent the believer from serving the Lord to his fullest potential. If one person is God-fearing and the other person is not, then there will be a temptation for you to sway toward the godless way of thinking or doing things, "evil communication corrupts good manners." (1 Corinthians 15:33) If you rush into a relationship with an unbeliever for a reason such as not wanting to be lonely, you may soon find out that you're just as lonely as you were previously, or you might start having a taste for the things of the world.

Marriage is a spiritual commitment. Take your time to find a partner who truly loves the Lord, whose heart yearns after righteousness. The scriptures say, "By their fruits, you shall know them." (Matthew 7:16) Young adults are especially tempted not to heed the commandment of being unequally yoked. When you meet someone to whom you are attracted to, you might say to yourself,

"I know so-and-so is not a Christian, but he'll become a Christian if I date him." Righteousness in one area is never a justification for sin in another. Time after time, single Christian men and women find themselves attracted to unbelieving men and women; they start as friends or even casual acquaintances. Think about this for a minute; a deceiver never alerts you to his true intentions until it is too late. Marriage between a believer and an unbeliever is like oil and water; they do not mix. Our world views are different; our moral standards are different; our lifestyles are different. Both are heading toward various destinations. You may ask, what if you marry someone, you thought was a Christian, but it turns out they are not. The unbeliever may appear to be open and tolerant at first, but as soon as the relationship is steady enough, he or she may take a stand against going to church, praying, or reading the Bible. I will share a story with you. A young lady got married to a man who turned out opposite to what he portrayed himself to be. He was calm, kind, and a lovely person while they were dating. He worked abroad, so their communication was via technology. They decided to get married after he visited her a few times. The lady migrated to the country where he resided to pursue her Ph.D. program. Then all hell broke loose; he was abusive, intolerant, and a liar. She suffered a miscarriage as a result of aggravated assault because she had what he considered an unwanted pregnancy. She found out he was already married; she had no choice but to divorce him.

I understand that sometimes you may grow anxious if you are not married by a certain age, or there is a lonely void in your life that nothing seems to fill. "The Lord said, "It is not good for man to be alone." (Genesis 2:18) He saw Adam's loneliness and provided him with a wife. We sometimes face the temptation to put God's words aside and follow what everyone else is doing. Authenticity and reliability are hard to find; this is the reason why we need to stick to the parameters God has provided for us.

## THE SAME HOUSEHOLD OF FAITH

*"Therefore, as we have opportunity, let us do good to all, especially to those who are of the household of faith."* (Galatians 6:10)

The same household of faith implies commonality in belief. Many people fall under the umbrella of Christianity, - Pentecostal, Roman Catholic, Methodist, Baptist, Presbyterian, Jehovah Witness, Mormon, etc. The Christendom is much divided on some doctrinal issues, which affect lifestyle and beliefs. Some churches encourage their ladies to dress modestly, no makeup, no earrings, no trousers, etc. If the couple attends the same church, they will be used to these doctrines, and it wouldn't be strange. But if the couple attends different churches, they might find some of these doctrines are unusual and strange. I will share a story with you. A couple was married in a Pentecostal church that they both attended. The man had been a member of the church for two years. He appeared to be a genuine Christian and faithful worker in the church. He approaches a lady in church, and they dated for about a year before they got married. On the wedding night, the man reveals to her he was not a Pentecostal Christian, but a member White garment church popularly known as the Celestial church. He wasn't interested in going back to the Pentecostal church as he had achieved his aim of marrying one of them. He concluded that there is no problem, she can continue to go to her church, but she must not interfere with his church activities, which include drinking alcohol. The lady felt like she was in a nightmare. Doctrinal issues are critical. As a matter of necessity, you must discuss your core doctrines with your partner before proceeding into marriage without compromising. When differences begin to surface, it breaks the unity of faith, and you will lose a tremendous amount of power. The scriptures say, "One shall chase a thousand, and two shall put ten thousand to flight." (Deuteronomy 32:30) Here are areas I would suggest you discuss:

1.  Salvation: What do you believe about Salvation? The role of Jesus in redemption, his substitutionary death on the cross that satisfied God's wrath as the payment for our sins. Do you believe there is no way to heaven except through him? (John 14:6)
2.  God's Word: What place does the Word of God occupy in your life, in this relationship, and ultimately the marriage? The inspiration and authority of the Bible; if someone denies this, there is no basis for determining what is spiritually true or false.
3.  The Holy Spirit, the third person in the trinity: Do you believe in the Holy Spirit and his role in the life of a believer?
4.  The Trinity: Do you believe God is one in essence and three in persona? God is one God who exists eternally as three co-equal persons, the Father, the Son, and the Holy Spirit, each of whom is entirely God.
5.  Prayers: Do you believe in the power of prayers?
6.  The future: Do you believe in Heaven and Hell?
7.  Baptism: Do you believe in water baptism and baptism of the Holy Spirit?

A discussion on doctrinal issues is not a show of whose doctrine is superior. It is an opportunity to help you and your partner understand each other's views on key issues and to gain clarity. There will be some grey areas; you have to determine which is minor and major; you might have to make concessions on minor issues. What is minor or major is determined by your personal convictions.

Churches under the umbrella of Pentecostal differ on key issues. For example, can a lady wear trousers? Should a lady cover her head in the church? Due to our propensity toward pride, it's easy to defend the truth in the wrong way, so try to understand what the other person is saying before you pass judgment. Be Gentle, Christian couples often have different levels of understanding the scriptures, but someone who is deliberately teaching false doctrine needs to be rebuked. If you get to a stalemate on major doctrine, seek the wisdom of others, including pastors or church leaders.

## REFLECTION QUESTIONS

1. Do you want children in the marriage? How many children do you want?
2. Do you have underlying medical issues?
3. How soon do you want to start having children after you get married?
4. Do you have a preference on the sex of the baby?
5. What are the core doctrines you believe?
6. What doctrinal issues would you classify as major versus important?

# PRAYER POINTS

1. Father, thank you for opening my mind to new wisdom in Your word
2. Father, by Your Holy Spirit, inspire me to ask the right questions in Jesus' name
3. Father, open my understanding and help me to uncover issues that can ruin my marriage
4. Father, help me not to compromise on my faith and calling in Jesus' name
5. Father, You are the healer, please, heal me of every hereditary disease in Jesus' name

# CHAPTER 8

# The Wedding Plan

Planning a wedding is one of the most exciting and enjoyable activity a couple can do together. It will be one of the first major projects they handle as a team. It is an opportunity to gain more insight into the person you are about to spend the rest of your life with. There are going to be difficult decisions and challenges, which can lead to disagreement. It could be as simple as the colour theme for the day, or as crucial as the location of the wedding. It will be divine if you agree with your fiancé at every wedding decision. The most important thing is that you learn to work together, if necessary, take days-off from the wedding planning to focus on other things, perhaps find something fun to do. During my wedding preparation, my wife and I went to an Amusement park for a day to take the load off. The point here is to have a plan in place in case the wedding plans start to take a toll on your relationship.

A wedding day has several vital participants, which are God, the church ministers, the bride, the bridegroom, the bridesmaids, the groomsmen, the families, vendors, and the guests. Each has a unique role that contributes to the success of the wedding day; your wedding day is not only about the couple. It's a great feeling of pride for parents to see their children get married. Although most of us have a dream about our wedding day, we must learn to accommodate others in our vision. Your parents especially want to be part of the wedding plans, sometimes with strong opinions on specific aspects of the wedding. Remember that they are coming from a place of love, and they're just as excited as you are. There is bound to be an area where all parties will have to compromise. Pick your battles carefully, so all sides feel as if they're a part of the event.

## THE BUDGET - WHO PAYS FOR WHAT?

*"Suppose one of you wants to build a tower. Won't you first sit down and estimate the cost to see if you have enough money to complete it?"* (Luke 14:28)

Couples in a serious relationship should have a vision for their wedding and how much it is going to cost. It puts both parties on the same page and avoids the fight that ensues between reality and fantasy. If you are fortunate to have parents who are willing to bankroll your wedding expenses, it takes the financial burden off you. You can use your funds for the deposit on a house if you have not bought one yet. Budgeting for a wedding can be a difficult task, particularly when one person has unrealistic expectations. If your fiancé plans to wear a ten thousand pounds designer wedding dress and your overall budget is thirty thousand pounds, then you have spent a third of your budget on just one item. The solution is to sit with your fiancé and come up with a number that the two of you are comfortable spending on a wedding, but let your number be realistic. Perhaps, do individual research before you both arrive at a figure for the wedding.

A different approach is to list (on a spreadsheet) everything you would both like for your wedding day, and then determine what is essential and what is not. The "bride to be" might choose to be responsible for a part of the list and the "groom to be" another part based on individual financial circumstances. If you are in the fortunate position that your parents have indicated their willingness to fund part or the entire wedding, then sit with both sets of parents or relatives and politely ask them what they would like to contribute toward the wedding. This rules out any false assumptions, and it helps you to know what is outstanding on your list. Remember to show gratitude to your parent or relative; it goes a long way when people commit to helping you financially. However, I must add that financial contributions sometimes come with strings. If your parent or relative is helping to foot the bill, you might find yourself in situations where they insist on their way, rather than help you accomplish your vision for your wedding day. If you can foresee this happening, you may want to consider limiting how much contribution you take from family.

Traditions affect the cost of the wedding and who pays for what. If your culture requires a wedding rite that lasts for a week, the cost would be substantially different compared to a simple engagement party and church blessing wedding style. Traditionally, the bride's family assumes most of the financial costs associated with a wedding. The bride's parents host the engagement party, and other costs are split between the two families. In some traditions, the Bride Price or Dowry is part of the wedding rites, so speak to your fiancé about their traditions. In most traditions, the groom's family pay the bride's price to the bride's family, but in some culture bride's family pays the groom's family; the amount can vary from a token to a significant sum.

As a rule of thumb, I advise against borrowing to pay for the wedding using credit cards, bank loans, etc. I don't believe the couple should start their lives with debt. However, weddings can be emotionally charged; this is a once in a lifetime event. If you are your parent's only child, it carries an additional burden. We all have different circumstances and difficult choices to make. It would be best if you controlled the finances for your wedding. I have seen a couple who had an emotional breakdown after their wedding due to the mountain of debt they had to deal with. The wedding is a single day, and marriage is a lifetime. Finally, always keep an "emergency fund" for yourself. There is bound to be an unforeseen expense that comes up.

## WEDDING VENUE - LOCATION, LOCATION, LOCATION

*"On the third day a wedding took place at Cana in Galilee."* (John 2:1)

Choosing a wedding location can be a challenging task, you might have a dream venue in mind that your partner disagrees with, or you are just starting your search as a couple. There are different variables to consider, from the availability of the location on a specific date, guests' willingness to travel for the occasion, to the seating plan, etc. Your wedding venue plays a critical role in the success of your wedding day. The choice of your wedding venue is one of the most crucial decisions you have to make with your partner. The question you probably have is, how do I choose a wedding venue? In this section, I aim to explore the variables that will help you make your choice.

I want to begin by asking you what your vision for your wedding day is? Do you have an image in mind of what your wedding day will look like? Have you seen a particular theme that you like, a picture, a brochure, a movie, etc.? Your vision will help you create the list of places to consider as a potential location for your wedding. There is the possibility that the list can be very long and also different from your fiancé. You might consider narrowing it down by asking yourself another question, what feels authentic to you or defines you as a couple? It could be the town or city you met and became a couple; it could the place you had your first date or the city he proposed, and you accepted. The venue should say this is who we are as a couple.

The second factor worth considering is the number of guests you are planning to invite. Couples often underestimate how many people will turn up for their wedding, and in an attempt to please everyone, they go over budget. When a venue is empty, it is sometimes hard to imagine how it will look when filled with tables and chairs, plus people. You might consider asking the venue manager for pictures of seating layouts or photographs of previous events held at the venue. These images will give you a good idea of how much space there is and the number of guests you can invite. The capacity of the room will affect the guest experience at your party; if the venue is too small, the party will feel too stuffy and overcrowded; if it is too big, they feel lost, and the space feels cold and empty.

The third factor to consider is asking each venue on your list if they are fully serviced, or do you have to bring your vendor for food, entertainment, and decorations. A place with tables, chairs, and linens might be considerably more expensive than a venue providing the bare minimum. If you decide to go for the bare minimum, consider carefully logistics and the costs of moving and removing rental chairs, tables, and linens, etc. This factor might add a considerable amount of money to the budget.

The fourth factor is where your guest will be coming from? If you choose a venue that is out of town, you must consider accessibility, accommodation, such as hotels within proximity to the venue. The reason is simple; road traffic could delay the start of the occasion. If some guests are coming from abroad, for example, parents or grandparents, how far is the closest international airport to the venue and the church? If you plan to use the same premises for both the church service and reception, how long does it take to turn the room around? What will the guests be doing while the room layout is changed? Perhaps they could be taking pictures with the couple and having light refreshments.

The fifth factor is the availability of the venue on a specific date. Certain times of the year are trendy for weddings, especially summertime. A popular venue might require one-year advance notice, and there might be a long waiting list. Some unscrupulous vendors might try to get into a bidding war, make sure you avoid this trap at all cost. If the venue you chose with your partner is non-negotiable, perhaps choosing a different date for the wedding might be the only viable option.

Undoubtedly seasons affect the weather. Having a wedding in summer means there is a high probability that there will be sunshine. Marrying in the spring or autumn means that there is a high probability of rain and high winds. For a couple planning to wear traditional outfits, you must consider the time of year you are planning the wedding. The weather affects the light, which is an important part of any event, especially wedding photographs.

Different towns and cities have different laws and ordinances. Ask your venue manager of any restrictions that govern your town. Some cities require a hall to be shut at a particular time, while others will cut out the music if it exceeds certain decibels. If the number of guests exceeds a certain amount, it will violate the fire code, or if you plan to bring alcohol on the premises, you might need a special licence. These are factors worth considering before choosing the suitability of the venue.

The sixth factor is Security and Parking for guests. Wedding crashers have no business being at your party. You might consider employing the service of crowd control, if not already provided by the venue, especially when there are restrictions to the number of people allowed in the hall. Wedding crashers often impact on the budget and enjoyment of your guests. Suppose the majority of your guest are within driving distance of your venue; they might choose to bring their car, so making provision for parking makes the wedding day more enjoyable for your guests.

The seventh factor is the budget. You have seen the venue and accessed the capacity. You know what services they provide. You also have a rough idea of the number of guests that are coming to the party. Now you have to decide with your partner which venue you've visited fits into your wedding budget. Some cost varies based on the number of people you're inviting for your special day. Your wedding day is a once in a lifetime event; this is the reason I have chosen to discuss the budget factor as the final topic to consider. The budget is made up of the choices you make for your wedding.

## WEDDING VENDORS - THE GOOD, THE BAD AND THE UGLY

When it comes to finding the right vendor for your wedding, it is not an exact science. With so many options available, it can be challenging to know where to start. The wedding industry is unregulated, and there is no uniformity in terms of services provided. It means vendors can get away with being unethical or providing poor service due to a lack of accountability. You can minimise your risk of falling into the wrong hands by doing your due diligence. Try consulting with locally married friends, speak to family or church members, and research social media recommendations, testimonials, or client referrals to assemble your wedding-day dream team.

Some vendors provide service contracts; I recommend that you have one in place with your chosen vendor, a simple service agreement that specifies the level of service expected, signed, and dated. It might entitle you to a refund or compensation if the service falls below expectations. Do not pay the full amount of money to any vendor except in exceptional circumstances; in most cases, a deposit should be all that is required. As a part of your due diligence, you might ask someone with a legal eye to go through the service policy with you.

Dealing with multiple wedding vendors can be the source of anxiety and frustration. Your vendors are experts who will bring your wedding vision to life—the ones who will make you cry tears of joy when you see their work. You might consider hiring a wedding coordinator to take the pressure off you. You will be dealing with one person as opposed to multiple people. One of the significant advantages of hiring an experienced wedding coordinator is having access to their network of wedding vendors. A good wedding coordinator will know the best decorators or where to get linen at the best price. Some wedding venues have a list of preferred vendors that they have tried and tested; this might help you narrow your search for your dream team. You might be fortunate to have a friend who is an expert at wedding planning and coordinating. He or she can contribute their talent to your big day, but ask them to be professional about it.

Don't be afraid to ask for a discount or negotiate on the price quoted by the vendor. The best way to accomplish this is to take the time to educate yourself on the market for a particular service. For example, you might ask for a quote from three or four vendors for the same quantity and quality of service. As a rule of thumb, take a day to consider or think before hiring a vendor. Ask for clarification if anything is unclear; for example, what's included in a quoted price, the vendor should itemize everything for you.

Finally, consider having an on-site wedding coordinator, so that the event will run smoothly and on time. The wedding coordinator duties will be helping to manage the various vendors at the venue. They will take charge of items on the day, such as the photography - the order in which the pictures will be taken so that no one is missed out, the food allocation to the tables, seating plan, etc. It will take the pressure off you so that you can have fun and enjoy your day.

## GUEST LIST AND SEATING PLAN

A common mistake made by the couple planning their wedding is that they invite more people than they can host at the venue. This often happens when you are trying to please everyone, especially couples with a large family, though it is understandable that it is difficult to exclude people. However, this can be a recipe for disaster. It is crucial that you know the venue's capacity before you send out the "Save the Date." Consider sending out your invite in batches and wait for them to be RSVPed before sending out more invites; this way, your guest list is controlled. As frustrating as it may seem, you will have to track guests down to see if they are coming to the wedding. You can delegate this task to a member of the family. Perhaps you might consider leveraging ready-made technology for people to RSVP and set reminders if they have not responded. There are times you may feel torn between decisions, like having an adults-only party or having children at the reception. Some of your friends or family members have children who need supervision. If the funds are available, you may have the best of both worlds by creating a fun space for the children and hiring an entertainer for them and still have your adult-only party. It will keep the kids at the party distracted and away from their parents. Your invite should include a section that allows a parent to indicate that their children are coming. There might be rules and regulations for the number of children allowed on the premises. It is wise to check with the venue manager.

The plus-one dilemma, this is another crucial point on a wedding invite. You extend plus-one invite to those friends or family who have a significant other, in a committed relationship, engaged, or married. Sometimes guests like to keep their plus-one open, which makes it difficult for your planning. You want to make sure that the unanticipated guest feels welcome; the solution is to encourage people to complete their RSVP by a specific date. Explain to them that your venue has a strict guest limit, and as much as you would love to have them all there, it isn't possible. Unfortunately, not everyone will understand that there was a cap on the number of guests you can have at the venue. Be prepared for the backlash from those not invited. There might be a few family or friends that make it a little harder than you expect. I have a family friend who has stopped speaking to me because I could not accommodate her and her five children at my wedding. There is no one-size-fits-all, but time is the best healer of wounds.

One of the trickiest aspects of planning a wedding is the seating plan. You cannot complete the seating plan without your guests completing their RSVP. How do you plan to seat aunts, uncles, nieces, cousins, work colleagues, next-door neighbours, etc., if you don't know if they are coming to the wedding? There are different variables to consider. For example, a family feud; Aunty Sally doesn't like Uncle Jo; they might start arguing at the party. Try approaching it in a systematic order, bride and groom, bridal party, both sets of parents, close family relatives, and then friends. Think of factors such as singles, brothers, and sisters, allow them to mingle at your party - you don't know what may happen. Try to strike a balance of male to female ratio at each table. It can be awkward if there is one man to eleven ladies on a table assuming there are twelve guests per table. Bear in mind people's interests and ages.

Finally, make sure you place the seating plan close to the entrance and the name of your guests well displayed; this will help them find their seats quickly and easily. Place the table name or number on the table. You can be creative with it; the names of the tables can be the countries or cities of the world you have visited. Don't forget to give a copy of your seating plan to the on-site wedding coordinator, in case of an emergency. I would recommend that you plan in some contingency for uninvited guests showing up, maybe plan in an empty seat at some tables.

## DON'T SKIP
## THE WEDDING REHEARSAL

Having a rehearsal before the big day could be one of the best decisions you make. Different church denominations have different rules for a wedding; a wedding rehearsal is an integral part of the wedding plan. It is usually organised a day or two before the wedding day.

It is an opportunity to get a feel and to work out the details of the wedding. If you are unsure, take the time to speak with the priest or officiating Minister before making any decision on the order of the day. In your discussion, ask what your options are and decide what elements you'd like to include in your ceremony and what you don't. Aside from the bride and groom, it is beneficial for the best man, groom's men, bridesmaids, parents, ushers, and the person walking the bride down the aisle to be at the rehearsal. It gives all the participants a chance to become familiar with the roles they will play on the big day. You want your wedding rehearsal filled with as much of your wedding party as possible. A run-through of it before the D-day will make it seem natural and help avoid some common pitfalls and awkwardness. It's an opportunity to settle the nerves and become familiar with when and where to walk, and where to sit or stand. Give some thought in advance to the following:

- Order of Procession (a typical wedding entrance is the bride and bride's father, bridesmaids and groomsmen in pairs except for the best man who remains at the altar with the groom)
- The pace of the walk (people rushing down the aisle might ruin photo moments or the timing of the walk to the beat of the music)
- The spacing between the bridal party
- Where the parents sit
- Where the bride and groom sit
- Where the wedding party sits, and what order do you want them to go in?
- Who carries the rings? This is an important job, decide beforehand who is responsible for your rings. If you have a child carrying your rings, make sure an adult oversees the responsibility of making sure they get to you at the right time. Hopefully, the best man doesn't forget where he has placed the wedding rings for safe-keeping.

- Who are the officiating Ministers? Do you want a guest minister from the groom's church?
- Order of recession, the exit: The couple recess together first, followed by the wedding party in pairs, and the officiating ministers, then the parents, who are generally sitting on the aisle in the front row followed by the rest of the guests.

This might sound a little complicated, but don't panic. There's no wrong answer to any of these questions, but you have to make a decision, don't assume things will be on autopilot.

## DEALING WITH UNCERTAINTIES

Planning a wedding comes with a lot of uncertainties and outside influence that could cause stress. I want to share a piece of advice given to me before my wedding, "the best way to enjoy the planning process and the day, is to realise that not everything will be the same way as you imagined it." You have to compromise a little, improvise a little, and forgive much. People will let you down, vendors might disappoint, events that you cannot control will happen. I stood outside the hall, waiting for my traditional engagement ceremony to begin when my relative walked up to me and whispered in my ear; he had dropped the engagement cake. I smiled and said, "It is ok." If I allowed that single event to ruin my day, I would have unpleasant memories of my wedding day for the rest of my life. I wrote it off as an event I could not control.

A factor you cannot control is the weather; there is no mathematical formula to avoid lousy weather, especially if you are having an open-air ceremony. My advice is; try and plan your day so that the show goes on no matter what is happening in the sky. Plan for every weather event, and make sure there is enough space for everyone indoors if it rains. Forecasts and predictions are helpful indicators, but there is no guarantee. Do not pick a destination or time of the year when the weather is generally bad. If possible, plan the event so that the weather is simply an added atmospheric feature rather than something to rely upon.

Dealing with the pressure of the wedding day and unforeseen circumstances is one of the crucial roles played by the wedding planner. He or She will be responsible for any last-minute changes or unexpected situations, like vehicles breaking down, bride's dress issues, or bridesmaids dress issues so that you can enjoy your day. They are expected to be vigilant, anticipating, and responding to any sudden changes with minimal fuss.

Another common fear is worrying that your guests won't enjoy the day, enjoy themselves too much, or they do not turn up at all. For your sanity, you need to know that you cannot fix everything that comes up. You cannot be upset or worried about your guests being bored or unhappy. If anyone has a history of letting you down, then are you sure you want them as a part of your wedding day. However, there are mitigating circumstances like people getting sick, cars breaking down, flights or trains are late or cancelled. If you're worried about someone drinking too much, speak to your wedding planner to find out how they might manage the situation. Generally, people will do everything possible to be there with you; they will surround you with love and goodwill on the day, so don't worry about a thing.

Finally, commit the day into the hands of God, the scriptures admonish us, "In all your ways acknowledge Him, and He shall direct your paths." (Proverbs 3:6) Raise a prayer altar for your day. A wedding is a big investment, and you need all the help you can get. Jesus performed His first miracle at the wedding in Cana (see John 2). I pray your wedding will be the all that you dream of and more in Jesus' precious name.

## REFLECTION QUESTIONS

1. Is your venue choice going to be used by multiple couples on the same day?
2. How much deposit is required?
3. Is there a payment schedule?
4. What is the cancellation policy? Do I get a full refund?
5. Who is the manager of the venue before, during, and after the wedding?
6. Are there additional hours available for clean-up, overtime, and early access into the venue? (Your decorators need a least two to three hours of decorating time)
7. Can you bring your home caterer to cook at the venue?

## PRAYER POINTS

1. Father, thank you for counting me worthy among those that will celebrate a wedding day
2. Father, visit my life with Your miracle and make my wedding day a glorious day
3. Father, let all forces in heaven and on earth co-operate together to make my wedding a success.

4. Father, raise up helpers for me on my wedding day.

5. Father, let the heaven be open, let there be abundance on my wedding day

Here is a list of vendors you might want to consider for the wedding plan

1. *Catering – Caterers*
2. *Do you want a set menu for the guest?*
3. *Wedding cakes*
4. *Makeup*
5. *Entertainment – Live music and DJ*
6. *Photography and Videographer*
7. *Decorations*
8. *Florist*
9. *Car hire*
10. *Hall hire*
11. *Wedding dress*
12. *Traditional attire dress marker*
13. *Suit hire*
14. *Wedding favours vendor*
15. *Transportation or rentals companies*

# CHAPTER 9

# Marriage Map

**M**arriage is not something that happens at the altar; it must be worked on daily. The expectations we bring into marriage will either bring failure or success. Remember, right-thinking brings right-action. The first year of marriage is the most challenging; a couple might experience emotional stress, financial insecurity, and unwanted relational influences as they try to navigate their pathway through life. These factors make it crucial to get a marriage map in place; it is a simple tool that helps the couple to get to where they are going. A marriage map should have been drawn before the "I do," so that both parties are on the same page on key issues, such as money, extended family, etc. When couples find themselves in unfamiliar crossroads during this early stage of their marriage, the choice of where to turn will be based on the marriage map they have designed together. The marriage map is designed with two primary purposes, "Where are we going with our marriage, and how do we get there? When couples work from the same page of their marriage map, they are better equipped to manage storms that come their way.

God's design for marriage is perfect. The husband is to be the head of his wife as Christ is the head of the church. The wife is to submit to her husband; this might not go down well with many women. A most modern school of thought would regard submission as chauvinistic, old fashioned, and out-dated. Ladies, worldly wisdom might say you are smarter, more qualified, and more educated with greater financial resources to lead the marriage than your husband. But God's words command that the husband should lead the marriage (see Ephesians 5:22 – 23). Humility is a crucial virtue for every believer. I recommend the book 'Love and Respect' by Dr. Emerson Eggerichs on this topic. I advise young ladies not to marry a man they do not respect. Likewise, I advise a young man who is not yet married to make sure he has the respect of his future wife before the "I do." A lady defined a perfect husband as one who cooperates with his wife's efforts to improve him. Ladies, your husband is not a puppy that needs to be trained.

Often young husbands abuse their privileged position of being the head of the home. They mistreat their wife by being a bully emotionally, physically, or even sexually, and he steps out of the realms of the scriptures; the union ceases to be scripturally based and managed. The husband is the head of the wife, means that he provides, protects, and supports his wife. Submission is difficult to define because we all have a different point of view on what submission should be - we are affected by our cultural background, education, and upbringing. Therefore, the word of God should be the standard. We often equate submission to weakness; historically, submission has been misused by men. I believe if you want to submit to your husband, then ask your husband, "What can I do to show you respect?" Your husband might say, "Don't put me down or criticize me in front of your friends and family," "Tell me I am still doing a good job even when I am struggling to provide for the family." Husbands should not demand submission; a wife's submission should be a natural act of her will when she can see God in the man she married. On the off chance that your husband tells you to do something that contradicts God's Word or will put you in harm's way, then you need to echo the words of Peter politely, "We must obey God rather than men." (Acts 5:29)

Finally, submission is based on the attitude of the heart, and not 'giving in' to the conquering force of another. It is the willing commitment to receive openly what the other has to offer. It was originally used in the military to refer to troops lining up in orderly arrangement. Submission carries the idea of entrusting oneself to the leadership of another to accomplish a task. It says nothing about the worth of a person, but rather the function with regard to the rest. The idea is that someone needs to take the lead or initiative, and the rest follow suit. In the marriage, the husband must take the lead, and his family follows him. He needs to be open to listening, willing to give himself for another's needs, and be sensitive and receptive to their values and overall vision. It is dangerous to marry a man without vision; it would be like trying to drive behind a parked car on the motorway.

# THE BLIND SIDE - BE A TEAM PLAYER

*"Above all, love each other deeply, because love covers over a multitude of sins."* (1 Peter 4:8)

In sports, the 'blind side' is one of the most vulnerable positions for an athlete because he cannot see when his opponent is coming, the player relies on his teammate to watch his back and to protect him. The blind side is also true of marriages; couples have areas in their lives where they most vulnerable. They must protect each other's blind side if the marriage is going to survive the storms. Couples must decide to tackle any troubles together. A husband must protect his wife from undue influences, especially his family, if they become overbearing on his wife. Trying to run an individual race in a marriage often spells disaster, it is like a passenger in a vehicle, thinking he or she is heading to a different destination from the driver.

Having a career goal is good, but if you fail to meet your spouse's most profound need, then the couple ceases from being a team. We mustn't allow our ego to lure us into a false sense of security. From time to time, we need comfort and encouragement from our teammate; if a wife keeps on nagging in the house, she might push her husband away from home. A simple illustration - two or more people can ride a car, but there is only one driver. If the passenger tries to be the driver, the vehicle will likely crash. I pray your marriage does not collapse during the tug-of-war that ensues between couples. Marriage is not a competition to see who the breadwinner can be; it is a partnership that lets the other person shine in the best possible light. It is easier to submit when you appreciate your partner's strengths and passions, be involved in letting it blossom so that others can benefit from your marriage.

The bible uses companionship to describe the relationship between a man and a woman. Companionship means the same team mentality, unlimited time for communion, and sharing your deepest hopes, dreams, and thoughts. Many people who have grown up watching their parent's marriage, who simply tolerated each other, have failed to grasp the concept of companionship. I have seen marriages ruined by couples who will talk about deep things or secrets with friends, parents, co-workers, work colleagues, and church members, but refuse to speak with their spouse. Becoming each other's closest life companion takes work, effort, and energy.

Stay connected by making one day a week for each other, just as God made the Sabbath a non-negotiable day for rest. It is to show us that there is more to life than work. Making an intentional effort to make at least one day a week makes your spouse feel special, allowing the couple to grow in the knowledge of each other. A consistent effort of spending a day with your spouse sharpens and stimulates your inner being, and the marriage stays colourful and bright.

## OUTSIDE HELP

*"Accept him who faith is weak, without passing judgment on disputable matters."* (Romans 14:1)

A cousin of mine shared her story with me; she said a day before her wedding, her mom called her to give her a piece of advice. Her mom said, "If you have any disagreement with your husband, please do not inform me." Her reason was that she couldn't see herself staying objective in a conflict between her daughter and her husband without being biased. She might support her daughter even if she is wrong. Long after the disagreement ended between the couple, she might still harbour resentment toward her daughter's husband. Some trials come your way that might be beyond your ability, experience, or resources to resolve. You must identify and agree who will be your go-to person with your spouse. It is easy to say, Mom and Dad. However, mom or dad can be biased or harbour resentment against your spouse long after you have settled the matter amicably. Your go-to person is someone who you can trust to tell you the truth, even if you don't like what they say. Running back to your parent at every hurdle might indicate that you need to cut the emotional umbilical cord or any other dependency, i.e., financial, or physical; you are to leave and cleave.

Ladies, men seem to be slow to figure out what they are supposed to do in their new role as a husband; some may never get it. Great wives are those who know how to deal with the daily annoying occurrence that eats away at the love in marriages. It takes some time for most women to figure out that men are not very motivated to do housework. You may discover your spouse watches television too much, and he does not help you enough with the housework. Don't magnify his imperfections until they drive you crazy. Learn to appreciate the hidden talents or gifts your partner has, and if they have not blossomed yet, encourage it to come out. Given time and the right encouragement, he might turn out to be the best husband and father. So, don't sweat the small stuff, enjoy the different gifts and talents of each other that you both bring into the marriage.

The bible encourages believers to work out their salvation with fear and trembling (see Philippians 2:12). In other words, some challenges do not have a ready-made answer. We need to work it out; this is especially true in new marriages. Marriages are similar to a house; when we enter into marriage, we have nothing. We slowly begin to build things together, share memories, and raise children. We make a home between ourselves and our spouses. External help might cause more rift than help to smoothen the rough hedges, especially if the assistance is one-sided, i.e., the mother in law, aunties, or uncles from one side of the family. Apostle Paul explained, "Do nothing out of selfish ambition or vain conceit, but in humility consider others better than yourselves. Each of you should look not only to your interests but also to the interests of others." (Philippian 2:3-4) Your spouse shouldn't feel that he or she is being ganged up against by members of your family.

## SHARED RESPONSIBILITY

Marriage is a partnership of shared responsibility and the willingness to share ourselves because the two lives become interwoven. In other words, what affects one person affects the other. A happy marriage does not come automatically; it must be worked at. It is a sacrificial process and not an instantaneous event. It doesn't happen merely because the preacher says, "I now pronounce you husband and wife," or because you signed a legal document. It is a lifelong process. We are all naturally self-centred. One woman complained to her marriage counsellor about her husband, "When he won a trip for two to Dubai, he went twice, by himself!" This is to highlight our self-centeredness.

Couples looking to make their marriage heaven on earth, need to sit together and make a list of the chores that must be done. Shared responsibility includes shared house chores. There will be a task on the list that you or your spouse might dislike doing. It could be ironing, cleaning dishes, or cooking; this list is a ground for negotiation. You might try the rock, paper, and scissor approach. If you carry the burdens all the time, sooner or later, as the burdens become increasingly heavy, you won't be able to carry on. A messy home might not bother some people, while others cannot stand the sight of a mess in the house. If you are comfortable with things being out of place, but your spouse is not, you both need to compromise by identifying what works best for both parties.

Becoming one is more than just sharing the same residence and bed. You will be hurt, disappointed, and offended by your spouse, and the only way you can recover is to practise something I call 'advance forgiveness.' In other words, before you hurt me, I have forgiven you. Just as you do not wish to destroy yourself and are quick to care for your wounds; so, you should take notice of any break in the peace of your marriage and quickly seek to heal it.

## DON'T UNDERESTIMATE THE POWER OF LITTLE THINGS

*"Catch for us the foxes, the little foxes that ruin the vineyards, our vineyards that are in bloom."* (Song of Solomon 2:15)

The husband and wife need to recognize that little things do matter; it creates an atmosphere of love and security for the couple. During courtship, couples tend to pay a lot of attention to each other, and they would consider their partner when they make plans. They wonder what the other person would think if they made a particular choice, they would try to look and smell their best. They talk on the phone for hours and can't wait for the moment when they are together once again. It seems that marriage has changed all that. Instead of paying attention to each other, they tend to find comfort in burying their faces in their phone or television.

Wives are more attuned to this than their husbands; men often let the little things slide. The accumulation of little things leads to frustration in marriage more than one big thing. It's like the difference between watering a flower every day or drowning it once a week.

When the couple finally talks about it, you hear this phrase: "I can't put my finger on it. We just sort of drifted apart." It is a lack of attention to the little things that can cause the drift. A bit more affection and a little more listening. A few more compliments when they come to your mind. A back rub now and then, saying, "I love you," a phone call in the middle of the day. A small surprise gift once in a while for no particular reason, planning a special night, or an occasional weekend getaway, preparing your husband's favourite meal, or taking your wife out for hers. A surprise love note left in a place your mate would not expect it. We're talking little things. You can use your imagination. The simple little thing goes a long way, and it enhances the couples' marital satisfaction and improves the quality of their relationships.

If you want your marriage to grow, remember that the little things matter. Communicate with your partner to learn what little things mean the most to them. You might have heard the phrase, 'men are from Mars, women are from Venus.' Couples are often not on the same wavelength; men don't pick up hints too well, ladies. If your husband asks what kind of little things you would like, please tell him as plainly as you can. For example, "I would like you to spend more time with me," "I would like to go to the restaurant twice a month." Women like to drop hints, but don't make him guess; tell him. Men don't get hints, be crystal clear, draw him a picture if you have to.

Finally, do you think because you have achieved a comfort zone with our spouse, it is time to get complacent? It is easy to take your spouse for granted than to do the little things that he or she would appreciate. Neglecting faithfulness in the little things can lead to big trouble. Remember, it's little things that lead to big changes.

## REFLECTION QUESTIONS

1. Are you comfortable discussing your deepest secret with your spouse?
2. Who is the go-to person in your marriage?
3. What role do you think a man should take in the family?
4. What role do you think a woman should take in the family?
5. What are the little things that your partner enjoyed during courtship?

# PRAYER POINTS

1. Father, thank you for the wonderful spouse you have given me.
2. Father, please help me to see where I am vulnerable, and protect me from being blind-sided in Jesus' name
3. Father, help me turn my home into heaven on earth in Jesus' name
4. Father, grant me the grace not to miss the little things in my marriage
5. Father, grant me the grace to outcast any destructive habit that could ruin my marriage.

# Final Words

*I* hope you have enjoyed reading this book, as much as I have enjoyed sharing the timeless principles of relationship with you.  My aim is to help you succeed in your choice of life partner. The principles in this book is to help you make informed decisions regardless of whatever stage you are in your relationship.

Throughout the scripture the church is often depicted as the Bride of Christ. I would also like to take this opportunity to invite you into the kingdom of God, if you are not already born again. It is the most important step you could ever take in life. You can make the decision to live for Jesus today by saying the prayer below.  After this, I recommend that you find a Bible believing church where you can become a member to grow in your relationship with Jesus Christ.

**Heavenly Father,**

*I come to you today as a sinner;*
*I believe your Word and in your Son Jesus,*
*that He died on the cross of Calvary*
*and on the third day He rose again from the dead*
*for my justification.*
*Today, I believe and confess*
*Jesus as my Lord and Saviour,*
*cleanse me of all my past sins by your blood.*
*I declare I am born again,*
*thank you Lord for saving me,*
*In Jesus name.*
*Amen.*

_______________________________________

Name:

_________________________

Date:

_______________________________________

Signed:

# Bibliography


**Benninger, M. (2019).** Know Your Love Language: Learn to Speak "Physical Touch" - Blinkist Magazine. [online] @blinkist. Available at: *https://www.blinkist.com/magazine/posts/love-language-physical-touch?utm_source=cpp* [Accessed 8 Apr. 2020].

**Buchanan, M. (2009).** The marriage delusion : the fraud of the rings? Lps Publishing.

**Chapman, G.D. (2004).** The five love languages : how to express heartfelt commitment to your mate. Chicago: Northfield Pub., C.

**Chapman, G.D. and Thomas, J. (2008).** The five languages of apology : how to experience healing in all your relationships. Chicago: Northfield Pub.

**Eggerichs, E. (2004).** Love & respect : the respect he desperately needs. Nashville, Tn: Integrity Publishers ; Colorado Springs, Colo.

**Endemano, S., Gibbs, O.E., Berry, S.R., Bice, D.A. and Schools, C. (1996).** One plus one : a Christian perspective on marriage and family. Colorado Springs, Colo.: Acsi.

**Feinberg, M. (2002).** A Single Womans Guide To Guarding Her Heart. [online] Growthtrac Ministries. Available at: https://www.marriagetrac.com/a-single-womans-guide-to-guarding-her-heart/.

**H Norman Wright (2004).** 101 Questions To Ask Before You Get Engaged. Eugene, Or.: Harvest House Publishers.

**Harley, W.F. (2013).** His needs, her needs participant's guide : building an affair-proof marriage (a six-session study). Grand Rapids, Mi: Revell.

**Larson, J.H. (2000).** Should we stay together? : a scientifically proven method for evaluating your relationship and improving its chances for long-term success. Editorial: San Francisco: Jossey-Bass.

**Leboeuf, M. (2000).** How to win customers and keep them for life : revised and updated for the digital age. New York: Berkley Books, Printing.

Lopez, K. (2018). Major Marriage Myths – 50/50. [online] Journey-christian.com. Available at: *https://journeychristian.com/major-marriage-myths-expectations-2/* [Accessed 9 Apr. 2020].

Martyn, E. and Relate (Organization (2003). Before you say "I do" : how to be happily married for ever! London: Vermilion.
Ramsey, D. (2010). The Total Money Makeover. Nashville, Tn: Nelson Current.

Rosberg, G. and Rosberg, B. (2002). Divorce proof your marriage. Wheaton, Ill.: Tyndale House Publishers.

Scott McCallum II, J. (2017). Reboot Your Marriage – First Hot Springs. [online] First Baptist Church, Hot Springs, AR. Available at: *https://firsthotsprings.com/sermons/reboot-your-marriage* [Accessed 28 Aug. 2020].

SermonCentral (2007). Ellen Petrakis. [online] Sermon Central. Available at: *https://www.sermoncentral.com/sermon-illustrations/61295/ellen-petrakis-by-sermoncentral* [Accessed 9 Apr. 2020].

Webber, R. (2012). Are You with the Right Mate? [online] Psychology Today. Available at: https://www.psychologytoday.com/us/articles/201201/are-you-the-right-mate [Accessed 26 Jan. 2018].

# OTHER TITLES
# FROM THE AUTHOR

Divine Strategies for
Invisible fight

Unwrapping Your
Redemptive Package